JOAN O

BY

LAURA E. RICHARDS

AUTHOR OF "FLORENCE NIGHTINGALE," "ABIGAIL ADAMS
AND HER TIMES," "ELIZABETH FRY," ETC.

D. APPLETON AND COMPANY
NEW YORK   LONDON

1919

JOAN OF ARC

TO

THE MEMORY OF

THEODORE ROOSEVELT

"ALSO A SOLDIER"

The extracts from "Joan of Arc," by Francis C. Lowell, are used by permission of Houghton Mifflin Company.

Selections from "The Maid of France," by Andrew Lang, are used by permission of Messrs. Longmans, Green & Co.

Theodosia Garrison's poem, "The Soul of Jeanne d'Arc," is reproduced by permission of Chas. Scribner's Sons.

CONTENTS

CHAPTER I

FRANCE IMPERISHABLE

THE SOUL OF JEANNE D'ARC

She came not into the Presence as a martyred saint
    might come,
  Crowned, white-robed and adoring, with very reverence dumb—
She stood as a straight young soldier, confident, gallant,
    strong,
  Who asks a boon of his captain in the sudden hush
    of the drum

She said "Now have I stayed too long in this my place
    of bliss,
With these glad dead that, comforted, forget what sorrow is
Upon that world whose stony stair they climbed to come
    to this

"But lo, a cry hath torn the peace wherein so long I
    stayed,
Like a trumpet's call at Heaven's wall from a herald
    unafraid,—
A million voices in one cry, '*Where is the Maid, the
    Maid?*'

I

JOAN OF ARC

"I had forgot from too much joy that olden task of mine,
But I have heard a certain word shatter the chant divine,
Have watched a banner glow and grow before mine eyes
  for sign.

"I would return to that my land flung in the teeth of war,
I would cast down my robe and crown that pleasure me
  no more,
And don the armor that I knew, the valiant sword I bore.

"And angels militant shall fling the gates of Heaven wide,
And souls new-dead whose lives were shed like leaves on
  war's red tide
Shall cross their swords above our heads and cheer us
  as we ride

"For with me goes that soldier saint, Saint Michael of
  the sword,
And I shall ride on his right side, a page beside his lord,
And men shall follow like swift blades to reap a sure
  reward

"Grant that I answer this my call, yea, though the end
  may be
The naked shame, the biting flame, the last, long agony;
I would go singing down that road where fagots wait
  for me

"Mine be the fire about my feet, the smoke above my
  head,
So might I glow, a torch to show the path my heroes
  tread,
My Captain! Oh, my Captain, let me go back!" she said.
                                        —*Theodosia Garrison.*

2

IN the fourth year of the Great War (1918), the sufferings of France, the immemorial battlefield of nations, were in all our hearts. We heard from time to time that France was "bled white"; that she had been injured past recovery; that she was dying. Students of History know better than this. France does not die She bleeds; yes! she has bled, and stanched her wounds and gone gloriously on, and bled again, since the days when Gaul and Iberian, Kymrian and Phoenician, Hun and Goth, raged and fought to and fro over the patient fields of the "pleasant land." Ask Caesar and Vercingetorix, Attila and Theodoric, Clovis and Charles the Hammer, if France can die, and hear their shadowy laughter! Wave after wave, sea upon sea, of blood and carnage, sweep over her; she remains imperishable. The sun of her day of glory never sets.

Her darkest day, perhaps, was that against which her brightest flower shines white. In telling, however briefly, the story of Joan the Maid, it is necessary to call back that day, in some ways so like our own; to see what was

3

the soil from which that flower sprang in all its radiant purity.

The Hundred Years' War prepared the soil; ploughed and harrowed, burned and pulverized: that war which began in 1340 with Edward III. of England's assuming the title of King of France and quartering the French arms with those of England; which ended in 1453 with the departure of the English from France, which they had meantime (in some part) ruled and harried. Their departure was due chiefly to the genius of a peasant girl of eighteen years.

France in the fifteenth century: what was it like?

King Charles VI. of France (to go back no further) whose reign Sully, "our own good Maximilian," calls "the grave of good laws and good morals in France," was not yet twelve years old when (in 1380) his father, Charles V., died. His majority had been fixed at fourteen, and for two years he was to remain under the guardianship of his four uncles, the Dukes of Anjou, Berry, Burgundy and Bourbon. With the fourth, his mother's brother, we have no concern, for he made little

4

trouble; the other three were instantly in dispute as to which should rule during the two years.

The struggle was a brief one; Philip of Burgundy, surnamed the Bold, was by far the ablest of the three. When the young king was crowned at Rheims (October 4th, 1380), Philip, without a word to anyone, sat him down at his nephew's side, thus asserting himself premier peer of France, a place which was to be held by him and his house for many a long day.

At seventeen, Charles was married (in the Cathedral of Amiens, the second jewel of France, where that of Rheims was the first) to Isabel of Bavaria, of infamous memory; and the first shadows began to darken around him.

The war with England was going on in a desultory fashion. Forty years had passed since Crécy. The Dukes of Lancaster and Gloucester, uncles and regents of Richard II., the young English king, were not the men to press matters, and Charles V. of France was wise enough to let well alone. The young king, however, and his Uncle Philip of Burgundy, thought it would be a fine thing to land

in England with a powerful army, and return
the bitter compliments paid by Edward III.
"Across the Channel!" was the cry, and preparations were made on a grand scale. In
September, 1386, thirteen hundred and eighty-
seven vessels, large and small, were collected
for the voyage; and Olivier de Clisson, Constable of France, built a wooden town which
was to be transported to England and rebuilt
after landing, "in such sort," says Froissart,
"that the lords might lodge therein and retire
at night, so as to be in safety from sudden
awakenings, and sleep in security." Along the
Flemish and Dutch coasts, vessels were loaded
by torchlight with "hay in casks, biscuits in
sacks, onions, peas, beans, barley, oats, candles,
gaiters, shoes, boots, spurs, iron, nails, culinary
utensils, and all things that can be used for the
service of man."[1] The Flemings and Hollanders
demanded instant payment and good prices.
"If you want us and our service," they said,
"pay us on the nail; otherwise we will be
neutral."[2]

The king was all impatience to embark, and

[1] Guizot, "Popular History of France," III, p 20
[2] Guizot, "Popular History of France," III, p. 21.

hung about his ship all day. "I am very eager to be off!" he would say. "I think I shall be a good sailor, for the sea does me no harm." One would have thought he was sailing round the world, instead of across the British Channel. Unfortunately for the would-be navigator, the Duke of Berry, for whom he was waiting, was not eager to be off: did not want to go at all, in fact; answered Charles's urgent letters with advice "not to take any trouble, but to amuse himself, for the matter would probably terminate otherwise than was imagined."[1] In mid-October, when the autumn storms were due, Uncle Berry appeared, and was met by reproaches. "But for you, uncle," exclaimed Charles, "I should have been in England by this time. If anyone goes," he added, "I will."

But no one went.

" 'One day when it was calm,' says the monk of St. Denis, 'the king, completely armed, went with his uncles aboard of the royal vessel; but the wind did not permit them to get more than two miles out to sea, but drove them back to the shore they had just left in spite of the sailors' efforts. The king, who saw with deep

7

displeasure his hopes thus frustrated, had orders given to his troops to go back, and at his departure, left, by the advice of his barons, some men-of-war to unload the fleet, and place it in a place of safety as soon as possible. But the enemy gave them no time to execute the order. As soon as the calm allowed the English to set sail, they bore down on the French, burned or took in tow to their own ports the most part of the fleet, carried off the supplies, and found two thousands casks full of wine, which sufficed a long while for the wants of England.' " [1]

Charles decided to let England alone for a while, and turned his thoughts elsewhere. He would visit Paris; he would make a Royal Progress through his dominions, would show himself king indeed, free from avuncular trammels. So said, so done. Paris received him with open arms; the king was good and gentle; people liked to see him passing along the street. He abated certain taxes, restored certain liberties; hopes and gratulations were in the air. He lodged in his palace at St. Paul, that home of luxury and tragedy, with "its

[1] Guizot, "Popular History of France," III, p 21

great ordered library, its carved reading-desks, its carefully painted books, and the perfumed silence that turns reading into a feast of all the senses,"[4] that palace "made for a time in which arms had passed from a game to a kind of cruel pageantry, and in which the search for beauty had ended in excess, and had made the decoration of life no longer ancillary to the main purpose of living, but an unconnected and insufficient end of itself."[1]

In this palace of his own building, Charles V. had died. Here his son grew up, handsome, amiable, flighty; here he brought his bride in the splendor of her then unsullied youth; here was born the prince for whom the Maid of France was to recover a lost kingdom.

After frolicking awhile with his good people of Paris, Charles started once more on his travels, and for six months wandered happily and expensively through his kingdom.

"When the king stopped anywhere, there were wanted for his own table, and for the maintenance of his following, six oxen, eighty sheep, thirty calves, seven hundred chickens, two hundred pigeons, and many other things

[1] Belloc, "Paris," p 248

9

besides. The expenses for the king were set down at two hundred and thirty livres a day, without counting the presents which the large towns felt bound to make him." [1]

Wherever he went, he heard tales of the bad government of his uncles; listened, promised amendment; those uncles remaining the while at home in much disquiet of mind. As the event turned out, their anxiety was needless. Charles's tragic fate was even then closing about him, and the power was soon to be in their hands again. In June, 1392, Olivier de Clisson was waylaid after banqueting with the king at St. Paul, stabbed by Peter de Craon, a cousin of the Duke of Brittany, and left for dead. The news coming suddenly to the king threw him into great agitation; the sight of his servant and friend, bathed in blood, added to his discomposure. He vowed revenge and declared instant war on the Duke of Brittany. In vain the other uncles sought to quiet his fury; his only reply was to summon them and his troops to Le Mans, and start with them on the fatal march to Brittany. It was in the great forest of Le Mans that the curse of the Valois, long

[1] Guizot, III, p 22.

foreshadowed, if men had had eyes to see, came upon the unhappy king. The heat was excessive; he was clad in heavy, clinging velvets and satins. He was twice startled, first by the appearance of a white-clad madman, who, springing out of the woods, grasped his horse by the bridle, crying, "Go no further! Thou art betrayed!" then by a sudden clash of steel, lance on helmet of a page overcome by the heat. At this harsh sound, the king was seen to shudder and crouch for an instant; then, drawing his sword and rising in his stirrups, he set spurs to his horse, crying, "Forward upon these traitors! They would deliver me up to the enemy!" He charged upon his terrified followers, who scattered in all directions. Several were wounded, and more than one actually killed by the king in his frenzy. None dared approach him; he rode furiously hither and thither, shouting and slashing, till when utterly exhausted, his chamberlain, William de Martel, was able to come up behind and throw his arms round the panting body. Charles was disarmed, lifted from his horse, laid on the ground. His brother and uncles hastened to him, but he did not recogniz them; his eyes were set, and he spoke no word.

"'We must go back to Le Mans,' said the Dukes of Berry and Burgundy; 'here is an end of the trip to Brittany.'

"On the way they fell in with a wagon drawn by oxen: in this they laid the King of France, having bound him for fear of a renewal of his frenzy, and so took him back, motionless and speechless, to the town." [1]

Thus began the agony which was to endure for thirty long years. There were lucid intervals, in which the poor king would beg pardon of all he might have injured in his frenzy: would ask to have his hunting-knife taken away, and cry to those about him, "If any of you, by I know not what witchcraft, be guilty of my sufferings, I adjure him in the name of Jesus Christ, to torment me no more. and to put an end to me forthwith without making me linger so." [2]

He did not know his false, beautiful wife, but was in terror of her. "What woman is this?" he would say. "What does she want? Save me from her!" [2]

At first every care was given him; but in

[1] Guizot, III, p 27   [2] Guizot, III, p. 28

12

1405, we find the poor soul being "fed like a dog, and allowed to fall ravenously upon his food. For five whole months he had not a change of clothes." [1] Finally someone was roused to shame and remorse at the piteous sight; he was washed, shaved, and decently clothed. It took twelve men to accomplish the task, but directly it was done, the poor soul became quiet, and even recognized some of those about him. Seeing Juvenal des Ursins, the Provost of Paris, he said, "Juvenal, let us not waste our time!"—surely one of the most piteous of recorded utterances.

The gleams of reason were few and feeble. In one of them, the king (in 1402) put the government of the realm into the hands of his brother, Louis, Duke of Orleans: Burgundy took fire at once, and the fight was on, a fight which only our own day can parallel.

We can but glance briefly at some of its principal features. In 1404 Philip the Bold of Burgundy (to whom we might apply Philip de Comines' verdict on Louis XI.: "in fine, for a prince, not so bad!") died, and his son John the Fearless ruled in his stead. His

[1] Guizot, III, p 29

reign began auspiciously. He inclined to push
the war with England; he went out of his
way to visit his cousin of Orleans. The two
princes dined together with the Duke of Berry;
took the holy communion together, parted with
mutual vows of friendship. Paris was edified,
and hoped for days of joyful peace. A few
nights after, as Orleans was returning from
dining with Queen Isabel, about eight in the
evening, singing and playing with his glove,
he was set upon by a band of armed men,
emissaries of Burgundy, and literally hacked
to pieces. Now all was confusion. The
poor king was told to be angry, and was furious: sentenced Burgundy to all m ner of
penances, and banished him or twenty years.
Unfortunately, Burg ily was at the moment
preparing to en' .r Paris as a conqueror.
Learning this, King, Queen, Dauphin and Court
fled to Tours, and Burgundy found no one in
Paris to conquer. This was awkward; the
king's suffering person was still a necessary ad-
junct toward ruling the kingdom. Burgundy
made overtures; begged pardon; prayed "my
lord of Orleans and my lords his brothers to
banish from their hearts all hatred and ven-

geance." The king was bidden to forgive my lord of Burgundy, and obeyed. A treaty was made; peace was declared; the king returned, and all Paris went out to meet him, shouting, *"Noel!"*

This was in 1409; that same year, Charles of Orleans, son of the murdered duke, lost his wife, Isabel of France, daughter of the king. A year later he married Bonne d'Armagnac, daughter of Bernard of that name, a Count of Southern France, bold, ambitious, unscrupulous. Count Bernard instantly took command of the Orleanist party, in the name of his son-in-law. He vowed revenge on Burgundy for the murder of Duke Louis, and called upon all good and true men to join his standard; thenceforward the party took his name, and Burgundian and Armagnac arrayed themselves against each other.

Now indeed, the evil time came upon France. She was cut literally in twain by the opposing factions. The hatred between them was not only traditional, but racial. Burgundy gathered under his banner all the northern people, those who spoke the *langue d'oil;* in the south, where the *langue d'oc* was spoken,

Gascon and Provençal flocked to the standard of Armagnac. Backward and forward over terrified France raged the ferocious soldiery. Count Bernard was a brutal savage, but he was a great captain. The Albrets and many another proud clan were ready to fight under his banner; the cause did not specially matter, so long as fighting and plunder were to be had. Among them, they formed the first infantry of France. Wherever they marched, terror ran before them. They summoned the peasantry to bind on the white cross of Armagnac; he who refused lost arm, leg, or life itself, on the spot. This method of recruiting proved eminently successful, and the Count soon had a goodly army.

John the Fearless of Burgundy ("who," says a French writer, "might better have been called John the Pitiless, since the only fear he was without was that of God") was hardly less ferocious than his enemy. In one battle he slew some thousands of unarmed citizens: in another he massacred twenty-five thousand Armagnacs at one stroke. One would really think it had been the twentieth century instead of the fifteenth.

Burgundy, cunning as well as ferocious, won over to his side first Queen Isabel, false as she was fair and frail; then the Kings of Sicily and Spain. Still seeking popularity, he besieged Calais, but was driven off by the English; finally he took possession of Paris and the king, and ruled both for a time with success and satisfaction.

Both parties did homage to Henry IV. of England (1399-1413), who took the provinces they offered and kept his own counsel.

, By and by there was trouble in Paris; the Butchers, a devout body, who carried axe or cleaver in one hand and rosary in the other, were scandalized by the dissolute habits of Louis the Dauphin and his followers; took it upon themselves to mend matters. They turned axe and cleaver upon the young courtiers; slew, tortured, imprisoned, at their will, with psalms and canticles on their lips. Moreover, encouraged by Burgundy, their friend and patron, they preached daily to the Dauphin, and a Carmelite monk of their following reproved him by the hour together. Bored and enraged, young Louis wrote to the Armagnacs, begging them to deliver him.

They rushed with joyous ferocity to the rescue. The Butchers were dispersed; Burgundy was forced to flee from Paris, leaving the jealously guarded person of the king in the hands of the enemy. The Orleanist princes entered Paris in triumph; everybody, everything, from the Dauphin himself to the images of Virgin and saints, was draped in the white scarf of the Armagnacs.

In 1414 a peace was patched up: it was agreed that neither the white scarf 'nor Burgundy's cross should be worn. Nothing special was said about the murdering, which seems to have gone on none the less, albeit less openly.

In 1413 Henry (IV.) of Lancaster died, and Henry (V.) of Monmouth reigned in his stead. The day of desultory warfare was over. Unhappy France, bleeding at every pore from the blows of her own children, must now face the might of England, led by one of the world's greatest captains. Torn by factions, weakened by loss of blood, ridden first by one furious free-booter and then another, what chance had she? Trembling, her people asked the question: the answer was Agincourt.

CHAPTER II

THE LION AND THE LILIES

"Fair stood the wind for France."—*Michael Drayton.*

I YIELD to no one in my love and admiration for Henry V. in his nobler aspects, but I am not writing his story now. He came to France, not as the debonair and joyous prince of our affections, but as a conqueror; came, he told the unhappy French, as the instrument of God, to punish them for their sins. The phrase may have sounded less mocking then than it does to-day. France knew all about the sins; she had suffered under them, almost to death; it seemed hard that she must bear the punishment too.

Neither John of Burgundy nor Bernard of Armagnac was at Agincourt. They hovered apart, two great eagles—or vultures, shall we say?—watching, ready to pounce when their moment struck. The battle lost and won, both chiefs made a dash for Paris and the king.

19

Armagnac made the better speed; Burgundy arrived to find his enemy, with six thousand fierce Gascons, already in possession of the city, king and Dauphin both in his hands, and he self-constituted Constable of France, in lieu of Charles d'Albret, slain in the great battle.

Savage though he was, Armagnac was a Frenchman, and a great captain. For some months he kept not only Burgundy but England at bay, holding the royal city against all comers. He even made a dash on Harfleur (now, 1415, in the hands of the English) which might have been successful but for the cowardice of some of his followers. He promptly hanged the cowards, but the moment was lost. Returning to Paris, he found the Burgundians making headway; banished, hanged, drowned, beheaded, right and left, imposed tremendous taxes, and for a time fancied himself, and seemed almost to be, virtual king of France.

It was only seeming; Burgundy's hour was at hand. Among those banished by Armagnac was Queen Isabel, whom (after drowning one of her lovers in a sack) he had sent off to prison in the castle of Tours. Down swept

THE LION AND THE LILIES

John the Fearless, carried her off, proclaimed her Regent, and in her name annulled the recent tax edicts. This was a mortal blow to Armagnac. His Gascons held Paris for him, but without money he could not hold them. Furious, he laid hands on whatever he could find; "borrowed" church vessels of gold and silver and melted them down to pay his men. All would not do. Paris now hated as much as it feared him and his Gascons. A little while, and hate, aided by treachery, triumphed over fear. One night the keys of the St. Germain gate were stolen from their keeper—some say by his own son. Eight hundred Burgundians crept in, headed by the Sire de l'Isle-Adam: crept, pounced, first on that Palace where Tragedy and Madness kept watch and watch; then, the king once in their hands, on the holders of the city. The Dauphin fled to the Bastille. Armagnac and his chief followers were betrayed and imprisoned. The banished Butchers returned, thirsting for blood. The hunt was up.

What followed was a foreshadowing of St. Bartholomew, of the Terror, of the Commune. Paris went mad, mad as her king in the forest of Le Mans. All day long frenzied bands, citizens and Burgundians together, roamed the streets, seizing and slaying; all night the tocsin rang, rousing the maddened people to still wilder delirium. On the night of June 12th, 1418, they broke open the prisons and murdered their inmates without discrimination; Armagnacs, debtors, bishops, State and political prisoners, even some of their own party; a slash across the throat was the kindest death they met. Count Bernard of Armagnac was among the first victims: for days his naked body hung on view in the Palace of Justice, while in the streets the Paris children played with the stripped corpses of his followers. Private grudge or public grievance could be revenged by merely raising the cry of "Armagnac." A sword swept, and the score was wiped out. Between midnight of Saturday the twelfth and Monday the fourteenth of June (1418) sixteen hundred persons were massacred in the prisons and streets of Paris.

So fell the Armagnacs: and in their fall dragged their opponents with them.

Paris streets were full of unburied corpses; Paris gutters ran blood; Paris larders were bare of food. The surviving Armagnacs, assembled at Melun, kept supplies from entering the city on one side, the English on the other. Hunger and Plague, hand in hand, stalked through the dreadful streets. Soon fifty thousand bodies were lying there, with no sword in their vitals. Men said that those who had hand in the recent massacres died first, with cries of despair on their lips. While the city crouched terror-stricken, certain priests arose, proclaiming the need of still more bloodshed; the sacrifice was not complete, they cried Two prisons still remained, the Grand Châtelet and the Bastille, crammed with prisoners; among them might be, doubtless were, Armagnacs held for ransom by the greedy Burgundians. To arms, once more!

Frenzied Paris responded, as—alas!—she has so often done. The public executioner, mounted on a great white horse, led the shouting mob first to one, then to the other great State Prison. Before the Bastille, John of Burgundy met them, imploring them to spare the prisoners; humbling himself even to take the hangman's bloody hand: in vain. All were slain, and the Duke had only the poor satisfaction of killing the executioner himself a few days later.

Bernard of Armagnac dead, Charles of Orleans safe, since Agincourt, in an English prison (writing, for his consolation and our delight, the rondels and triolets which will keep his name bright and fresh while Poesy endures), John the Fearless was in very truth virtual king of France. Being so, it behooved him to make some head against Henry of England, who was now besieging Rouen. This was awkward for John, as he had for some time been Henry's secret ally, but Rouen was in extremity, Paris in danger; even his own faithful followers began to look askance and to demand active measures against perfidious and all-conquering Albion. John temporized by sending four thousand horsemen to Rouen, weakening by just so much his hold on the capital. He dared not declare himself openly on the side of England; dared only make a secret treaty with Henry, recognizing his claim to the French crown.

Before setting out from England to besiege Rouen, Henry had paid friendly visits to his prisoner-kinsmen, the Dukes of Orleans and

Bourbon, and succeeded in alarming both thoroughly. "Fair cousin," he said to the latter, "I am returning to the war, and this time I shall spare nothing: yes, this time France must pay the piper!" and again, perhaps to Orleans this time, "Fair cousin, soon I am going to Paris. It is a great pity, for they are a brave people; but, *voyez vous*, they are so terribly divided that they can do nothing."

Ominous words for a young gentleman to hear who was just writing, perhaps, that he would no longer be the servant of Melancholy.

> "Serviteur plus de vous, Merencolie,
> Je ne serez car trop fort y travaille!"

Rondel and triolet were laid aside, and the two princes wrote urgent letters to their cousin Charles, imploring him to make peace on Henry's own conditions: poor Charles, who did not know his own name or the names of his children, who still whispered, "Who is that woman? Save me from her!"

Meantime Henry sent his own messengers, in the shape of some eight thousand famishing Irishmen, whom he carried across the Channel and—*dumped* seems the fitting word—

in Normandy, bidding them forage for themselves. Unarmed, but fearing nothing, and very hungry, the Irish roamed the country mounted on ponies or cows, whichever was "handy by," seeking what they might devour. Monstrelêt describes them; may have seen them with his own eyes. "One foot was shod, the other naked, and they had no breeches. They stole little children from the cradle, and rode off on cows, carrying the said children"; to hold them for ransom, be it said.

My little measure will not hold the siege of Rouen. It was one of the terrible sieges of history, and those who love Henry of Monmouth must read of it with heavy hearts. In January, 1419, when fifty thousand people were dead of famine in and around the city, submission was made. Henry entered the town, with no doubt in his own mind and little in those of others, as to who was actually King of France.

He found the kingdom still rent in twain. The Dauphin Louis was dead, and Charles, his younger brother, had succeeded to the title and to the leadership of the Orleans party. The weak, irresolute, hot-headed boy of sixteen was

26

surrounded by reckless Gascons who lived by their swords and wits, caring little what they did, so money might be got, yet who were Frenchmen and had red blood in their veins. The peace now openly concluded between Henry and Burgundy roused them to frenzy. English rule was not to their mind. They beset the Dauphin with clamors for revenge to which he lent only too willing an ear. The affair was arranged, and as in the case of the murder of Orleans twelve years before, began with a reconciliation. The Dauphin longed to see his dear cousin of Burgundy; begged that they might meet; suggested the Bridge of Montereau as a fitting place for the interview. With some misgivings, the Duke consented, spite of the warnings of his friends. "Remember Louis of Orleans!" they said. "Remember Bernard of Armagnac! Be sure that those others remember them well!"

John the Fearless answered as became his reputation. It was his duty, he said, to obtain peace, even at the risk of his own life. If they killed him, he would die a martyr: if not, peace being secured, he would take the Dauphin's men and go fight the English. Then they

should see which was the better man, Han-
notin (Jack) of Flanders or Henry of
England.

On the tenth of September (1419), he
reached Montereau, and the long crooked
bridge spanning the broad Seine. Over the
bridge the Orleanists had built a roof, trans-
forming it into a long gallery: in the centre,
a lodge of rough planks, a narrow door on
either side. This was the place of rendezvous,
where the Dauphin awaited his visitor. The
Burgundian retainers disliked the look of it, and
besought their master not to set foot on the
bridge. Let the Dauphin meet him on dry land,
they said, not on a crazy bridge over deep water.
The Duke, partly of his own bold will, partly
through the wiles of a treacherous woman set
on by his enemies, laughed at their entreaties;
entered the bridge as gayly as he had entered
that Paris street, hardly wider than this foot-
way, where he had looked on at the murder of
Louis of Orleans, twelve years before.

"Here is the man I trust!" he said, and
clapped the shoulder of Tanneguy Duchâtel,
who had come to lead him into the trap. Ten
minutes later, and he was lying as Orleans had

lain, hacked in pieces, while the Orleanists exulted over his body as he had done over that of their leader.

I do not know that there is much to choose between these two murders, or that we need greatly sorrow for either victim. Probably neither gentleman would be at large, had he lived in our time.

And now Henry of Monmouth was king indeed. A few months, and the Treaty of Troyes was signed, and Henry entered Paris in triumph, riding between King Charles (who whispered and muttered and knew little about the matter) and the new Duke of Burgundy, Philip the Good, son of the murdered man. To that ill-omened Palace of St. Paul they rode, and there lodged together for a while. Henry's banner bore the device of a fox's brush, "in which," says Monstrelêt, the chronicler, "the wise noted many things." Henry had long been a hunter of the fox; now he came to hunt the French. Paris, still torn and bleeding from the wounds of opposing factions, welcomed anything that looked like peace with power; justice was not looked for in those days. Yet it was in the name of Justice that the two kings, sitting side by side on the same throne, heard the solemn appeal of Philip of Burgundy and his mother for judgment upon the murderers of John the Fearless. They demanded that the *soi-disant* Dauphin, Duchâtel and the other assassins of the Duke, in garb of penance and torch in hand, should be dragged in tumbrils round the city, in token of their shame and their repentance. The Estates of the Realm, summoned in haste, and the University of Paris, supported the demand; the two kings agreed to it. Nothing was needed save the culprits themselves, but they were not forthcoming. Appear before King and Parliament to receive his just doom? The Dauphin thanked them! If the King of England could play the hunter, Charles of Valois could play the fox; *et voilà tout!* "I appeal," said the Dauphin, "to the sharp end of my sword!" Thereupon he was denounced as a treacherous assassin, to be deprived of all rights to the Crown and of all property. The confiscation extended to his followers, and to all the Armagnac party, living or dead; and the good citizens of Paris, fleeced to the bare skin, helped themselves as best they might from the possessions of the outlawed Prince and his recreant nobles.

The Palace of St. Paul saw in those days the soldier-wooing of Henry V. and his wedding to Catherine of Valois, the daughter of Charles VI.: saw, two years later, the death of Charles himself, who faded out of life some two months after his great conqueror; later still, in one of its obscure chambers, neglected and despairing, the death of Isabel of Bavaria. After that it saw little of note, for people avoided it; it was an unlucky place, haunted forever by those twin shadows of Madness and Terror. Gradually it crumbled, passed finally into the dimness of forgotten things. To-day no stone of it stands upon another.

CHAPTER III

DOMRÉMY

"Quand j'étais chez mon père, petite Jeanneton . . ."

"I THOUGHT this was a life of Joan of Arc!" some bewildered reader may protest. "I don't want to read a History of France!"

Patience, gentle one! the Maid and her France may not be separated.

Now, however, it is time to go back a little to the year 1412, and make our way to the village of Domrémy on the banks of the Meuse, near the border of Lorraine.

Domrémy is not an important place: it has to-day, as it had four hundred years ago, about forty or fifty houses. It lies pleasantly enough by the river side, amid green meadows; a straggling line of stone cottages, with roofs of thatch or tile; behind it rise low hills, now bare, once covered with forests of oak and beech. Its people are, as they have always been,

grave and God-fearing; there is a saying about
them that they "seldom die and never lie."
They have always been farming people, growing corn, planting vineyards, raising cattle. In
old times, as to-day, the cattle fed on the rich
pastures of the river valley; the village children
tended them by day, and at nightfall drove
them back to the little stone-walled farms.

The houses were "small, of one or two or
three rooms, and sometimes there was a low
garret overhead. The furniture was simple:
a few stools and benches, a table or a pair of
trestles with a board to cover them, a few pots
and pans of copper, and some pewter dishes.
The housewife had in her chest two or three
sheets for her feather-bed, two or three ker-
chiefs, a cloak, a piece of cloth ready to be
made into whatever garment was most needed,
and a few buttons and pins. Often there was
a sword in the corner, or a spear or an arblast,
but the peasants were peaceful, seldom waged
war, and often were unable even to resist
attack."[1]

The people of Domrémy were vassals of
the lords of Bourlemont, whose castle still

[1] Lowell "Joan of Arc," p 15.

overlooks the Meuse valley. The relationship was a friendly one in the main. The dues were heavy, to be sure. "Twice a year a tax must be paid on each animal drawing a cart; the lord's harvest must be gathered, his hay cut and stored, firewood drawn to his house, fowls and beef and bacon furnished to his table. Those who had no carts must carry his letters." [1]

But this was the common lot of French peasants. In return, the lord of Bourlemont recognized certain responsibilities for them in time of trouble. His own castle was four miles distant, but in the village itself he owned a little fortress called the Castle of the Island, which the villagers guarded for him in time of peace and where they could take refuge in time of danger. Sometimes even, the Seigneur seems to have had pangs of conscience concerning his villagers, as when, in 1399, the then lord provided in his will that "if the people of Domrémy can show that they have been unjustly compelled to give him two dozen goslings, restitution shall be made." [2]

[1] Lowell "Joan of Arc," p 18.
[2] Luce "Jeanne d'Arc à Domrémy," p 19.

In one of the stone cottages (standing still, though overmuch restored) lived, early in the fifteenth century, Jacques d'Arc and Isabel his wife. Jacques was a responsible man, liked and respected by his neighbors. As dean of the village, he inspected weights and measures, commanded the watch, collected the taxes. Dame Isabel had enough learning to teach her five children their *Credo*, *Pater* and *Ave*, but probably little more; she spun and wove, and was doubtless a good house-mother. With four of the children we have little concern; our affair is with the fifth, a daughter born (probably) in January, 1412, and named Jeanne or Jehane. All her names are beautiful: "Jeanne la Pucelle," "the Maid of Orleans," "the Maid of France"; most familiar of all to our Anglo-Saxon ears, "Joan of Arc."

Joan was three years old when Agincourt was lost and won. It was a far cry from upper Normandy to the province of Bar where Domrémy lay; the Meuse flowed tranquilly by, but no echoes of the English war reached it at this time. Life went peacefully on; the children, as I have said, drove the cattle to the river meadows, frolicked beside the clear stream, gathering flowers, singing the immemorial songs of France; and as evening closed, drove them home again to the farm: or they tended their sheep on the Common, or followed their pigs through the oak forest that stretched behind and above it. In the forest lurked romance and adventure, possible danger. There were wolves there; no doubt about that. There were also, most people thought, fairies, both good and bad. Near the village itself stood the great beech tree known as "the Ladies' Tree," or the "Fairies' Tree," with its fountain close by, the Fountain of the Gooseberry Bushes, where people came to be healed of various diseases. Another great tree was called *"Le Beau Mai,"* and was even more mystical. Who knows from what far Druid time came the custom of dancing around its huge trunk and hanging garlands on its gnarled boughs? They were pious garlands now, dedicated to Our Lady of Domrémy; but it was whispered that the fairies still held their revels there. The lord of Bourlemont and his lady sometimes joined the dancing; had not his ancestor loved a fairy when time was, and been loved of her? They never

failed to join the rustic festival that was held
under the Fairy Tree on the "Sunday in Lent
called *Laetere*, or *des Fontaines*." One of
Joan's godmothers said she had seen the
fairies: Joan never did. She hung garlands,
with the other little girls; danced with them
hand in hand, singing. One would like to
know the songs they sang. Was one of them
the quaint ditty whose opening lines head this
chapter?

> *"Quand j'étais chez mon père, petite Jeanneton,*
> *La glin glon glon,*
> *M'envôit a la fontaine pour remplir mon cruchon!"*

Or was it the story of that *vigneron* who had
a daughter whom he would give to neither
poor nor rich, *lon la*, and whom he finally saw
carried off by a cavalier of Hungary,

> *"La prit et l'importa,*
> *Sur son cheval d'Hongrie, lon la!"*

A warning to selfish Papas. Or did there come
to Domrémy, wandering down the Meuse as
the wind wanders, some of those wild, melancholy sea-songs that the Corsairs and the fisher-

men sang, as they sharpened their cutlasses or drew their nets in harbor?

"Il était trois mâtelots de Grois,
Embarqués sur le Saint Francois,
Tra la derida la la la!"

Olivier Basselin, of Val-de-Vire, died when Joan was six years old, but his songs are alive to-day: gay little songs, called from the place of their origin *"Vaux-de-Vire,"* whence the modern word *vaudeville.* Perhaps Joan and her playmates sang his songs; I do not know.

In later, sadder years, Joan's enemies made, as we shall see, all that could be made out of these simple woodland frolics. *"Le Beau Mai,"* which in spring was "fair as lily flowers, the leaves and branches sweeping the ground" [1] became a tree of doom, a gathering-place of witches, of worse than witches. Joan herself, hanging her pretty garlands to the Virgin, as sweet a child-figure as lives in history, became a dark sorceress, ringed with flame, summoning to her aid the fiends of the pit. We need not yet turn that page; we may see her as her neighbors saw her, a grave,

[1] Gerardin

brown-eyed child, beloved by old and young: industrious, as all her people were; guiding the plough, watching the sheep or cattle, gathering flowers, acorns, fagots: or indoors, spinning, sewing, learning all household work under her mother's guidance. She loved to go to church, and hastened thither when the bell rang for mass; preferring it to dance or play.

"There was not a better girl," the neighbors said, "in the two villages (Domrémy and Greux). For the love of God she gave alms; and if she had money would have given it to the *curé* for masses to be said."

The village beadle being a trifle lax in his ways, she would bribe him with little presents to ring the church bell punctually. The children did not always understand her, would laugh sometimes when she left the games and went to kneel in the little gray church; but the sick and the poor understood her well enough. She loved nursing, and had a light hand with the sick; they never forgot her care of them; it was her way, if any poor homeless body came wandering by (there were many such in France then, almost as many as to-day) to give up her bed to the vagrant and sleep on the hearth all night.

Joan was eight years old when the Treaty of Troyes was signed, by which France virtually passed into the hands of England. Not long after, the miseries of war invaded the quiet valley of the Meuse; Burgundian and Armagnac began to burn, harry and slay here as they had long been doing elsewhere. The latter were headed by Stephen de Vignolles, better known as La Hire, a man as brave as he was brutal, and with a spark of humor which lights his name yet on the clouded page of the time. It is told how one day, starting out to relieve Montargis, besieged by the English, he met a priest on the way, and thinking it might be well to add spiritual armor to "helm and hauberk's twisted mail," demanded absolution. The priest demurred; confession must come first. "I have no time for that!" said La Hire, "I'm in a hurry; I have done in the way of sins all that men of war are in the habit of doing." "Whereupon," says the chronicler, "the chaplain gave him absolution for what it was worth, and the knight, putting his hands together, prayed thus, 'God, I pray thee to do

for La Hire this day as much as thou wouldest
have La Hire do for thee if he were God
and thou La Hire!'"

Similar stories are told of many men in many
lands; this may be as true as the rest of them.

La Hire's valiant doings by the side of Joan
and Dunois at Orleans and elsewhere, are on
the credit side of his book of life; but in the
years following 1420, he and his like wrought
dreadful havoc in the valley of the Meuse.
They pretended to seek redress for hostile acts;
in reality, they wanted blood and plunder, and
took both without stint. They drove off the
cattle and burned the crops; this was the least
of it. "These men," wrote Juvenal des Ursins,
"under pretence of blackmail and so forth,
seized men, women, and little children, regard-
less of age and sex; violated women and girls;
killed husbands and fathers before their wives
and daughters; carried off nurses, and left their
children to die of hunger; seized priests and
monks, put them to the torture, and beat them
until they were maimed or driven mad. Some
they roasted, dashed out the teeth of others,
and others they beat with great clubs. God
knows what cruelty they wrought."

Jacques d'Arc and another man of means (as means went in Domrémy!) hired the Castle of the Island from the lady of Bourlemont, at a considerable rent, for the safekeeping of their families and their flocks and herds in case of attack. A year or two later, the men of Domrémy bound themselves to pay a hearth-tax to the lord of Commercy, a highborn ruffian of the neighborhood, so long as he abstained from burning and pillaging their homes. The bond declares itself to be given "with good will, and without any force, constraint, or guile whatsoever." No need for an Artemas Ward to add, "This is rote sarkasticul!" The villagers knew well enough that if the blackmail were not paid, houses, church and all would go up in smoke and flame.

Joan, as she herself says, "helped well to drive the cattle and sheep to the Island," when news came of raiders prowling up or down the valley. Burgundian or Armagnac, it mattered little which; neither boded any good to the village. The Castle itself was uninhabited: its blank windows looked down on a garden, with great poplar trees here and there, and neglected flower-beds, once the delight of the Lady and

her children. Bees hummed in the lilies, birds
flitted from branch to branch, caring nothing
for Burgundian or Armagnac; all was peace
and tranquillity. Here the dreamy child wandered, looking up at the silent walls, seeing in
thought, it may be, shadowy figures of knight
and lady gazing down on her, the child of
France who was to be her country's saviour.

Doubtless she watched the boys playing at
siege and battle in and around the little fortress:
for aught we know, she may have joined their
play, and so learned her first lessons in arms.
In any case, tales of blood and rapine must
have been daily in her ears; emphasized about
this time by news of the death of a cousin,
"struck by a ball or stone from a gun."

Other tales were doubtless in her ears.
Among the wanderers who sat by the kindly
fireside of Jacques d'Arc would be mendicant
friars, Franciscan or Cordelier, making their
way from door to door, from village to village,
giving in return for food and shelter what they
had to give: a blessing for the hospitable house,
a prayer for its inmates, and news of the countryside. The last raid discussed, the next
prognosticated, the general state of country

and world deplored, there might be talk of things spiritual. The d'Arc family would naturally tell of their patron St. Rémy, who, watching over the holy city of Rheims, was so kind as to extend his protection over Domrémy. What a learned, what a wonderful man! how bold in his admonition to King Clovis at the latter's baptism! "Bow thy head meekly, O Sicambrian! adore what thou hast burnt, and burn what thou hast adored!" Yes! yes! brave words!

Then the guest might ask, was not this the country of the Oak Wood, *"le Bois Chesnu?"* Had they heard the prophecy that a Maid should be born in the neighborhood, who should do great deeds? Yes, truly, there was such a prophecy. It was made by Merlin the Wise. In Latin he made it; *Nemus Canutum*, the place; surely an oak wood, on the borders of Lorraine. That was long and long ago, and had been well-nigh forgotten; but a generation ago only—surely they had heard this?—a holy woman, Marie of Avignon, had made her way to his sacred Majesty, then suffering cruelly under the dispensations of God and also under that wicked Queen Isabeau, on whom might his sufferings be avenged, amen! made her way to him, and told of a dream she had dreamed, a terrible dream, full of clashing of swords. She saw shining armor, and cried out, alas! she could not use it! but a voice said that it was for a Maid who should restore France. Yes, indeed, that would be a fine thing, if our fair country, ruined by a woman, should be restored by a woman from the marches of Lorraine. *Pax vobiscum!*

These things, and others like them, no doubt Joan heard, sitting quietly by with her sewing or knitting while the elders talked. These things by and by were to be a sword in her hand, and—later still—a torch in the hands of her enemies.

CHAPTER IV

GRAPES OF WRATH

"In Rama was there a voice heard, lamentation, and weeping, and great mourning. Rachel weeping for her children, and would not be comforted, because they are not."—*Jeremiah.*

WHEN the conqueror of Agincourt lay dying at Meaux, word was brought to him that his queen, Catherine of France, had borne him a son at Windsor Castle. "Alas!" he said; "Henry of Monmouth has reigned a short time and conquered much. Henry of Windsor will reign long and lose all." Few prophecies, perhaps, have been so literally fulfilled.

At the accession of Henry VI., the "meek usurper,"[1] France was as near her death-agony

---

[1] "Ye towers of Julius, London's lasting shame,
With many a foul and midnight murder fed,
Revere his Consort's faith, his Father's fame,
And spare the meek usurper's holy head!"
—*Gray*, the Bard.

as she had ever been. Since the first invasion of Henry V., war, famine and pestilence had never ceased their ravages. Whole districts, once peopled, had become solitary wastes. The peasants, tired of sowing that others might reap, threw down pick and hoe, left wife and children, in a despair that was near to madness, and took to the woods, there to worship Satan in very truth. God and his saints having forsaken them, they would see what Satan and his demons could do for them. Things could not be worse, and at least in this service they would stand where their masters and tyrants stood.

In Paris, things were no better. In the year 1418 there died in the city of the plague alone, 80,000 persons. "They are buried in layers of thirty and forty corpses together, packed as bacon is." [1]

Two years later, when the English entered Paris, it was hoped that they would bring with them not only peace and order, but food. The hope was vain. "All through Paris you could hear the pitiable lamentation of the little children. One saw upon one dungheap twenty,

[1] "Journal of a citizen of Paris."

thirty children dying of hunger and cold. No
heart was so hard but had great pity upon hearing their piteous cry throughout the night, 'I
die of starvation!' " [1]

By day, when the dog-killer passed through
the streets, he was followed by a throng of
famished people, who fell upon each stray dog
as it was killed, and devoured it, leaving the
bare bones: by night the wolves, also hungry,
the country being stripped, made their way into
the city, where they found ample provender
in the scarcely-covered corpses.

A kind of death-madness sprang up and
seized upon the people; a hideous carnival of
corruption began. People danced, as in the
fairy-tales, whether they would or no, sick and
well, young and old, and their dancing-green
was the graveyard. A grinning skeleton was
enthroned as King Death, and round him the
frantic people danced hand in hand, shouting
and singing, over the graves that held their
friends and kinsfolk. Soon there was no more
room in the burial places; but still the people
died. Charnel houses were built, where corpses
were stored, being taken up a short time after

[1] "Journal of a Citizen of Paris"

burial to make room for fresh ones. The soil of the Cemetery of the Innocents was piled eight feet high above the surrounding streets.

Such was life—and death—for the common people, whom no man regarded. We have already seen how it was with the noble in war; in private life they were no less fanatic. That strange and hideous phenomenon known as the blood-madness of tyrants, broke out like some frightful growth upon the unhappy country. The chronicles of the time read like records of nightmare. Great princes, noble knights, robbed, tortured, slew their wives, fathers, brothers, no man saying them nay. The Sieur de Giac gave his wife poison, and made her gallop on horseback behind him till she dropped dead from the saddle. Adolf de Gueldres, "under the excuse that parricide was the rule in the family," dragged his father from his bed, compelled him to walk naked five miles, and then threw him down into a horrible dungeon to die.[1] The time was past when the *"prudhommes,"* the honest men of a village, might come before their lord and rebuke

[1] Lt-Col A. C. P Haggard, D S O "The France of Joan of Arc"

him with "Messire, such and such a thing is not the custom of the good people of these parts!" In the fourteenth century, they were listened to; in the fifteenth, they would probably have their throats cut and be thrown on the dungheap.

> "Of the same lump (as it is said)
> For honor and dishonor made,
> Two sister vessels"

Say rather, of the same earth two flowers. From the same dreadful soil of carnage that gave birth to the Lily of France springs up to enduring infamy a supreme Flower of Evil, the figure of Gilles de Rais, Marshal of France. His story reads like a fairy tale gone bad.

Born in 1404, grandnephew of Bertrand du Guesclin, neighbor and relative of Olivier de Clisson; comrade-in-arms of Joan of Arc. Orphaned in his boyhood, he was left to the over-tender mercies of an adoring grandfather who refused him nothing. In after years, when horror closed round his once-shining name and men shrank from him as from a leper, he cried out in his agony: "Fathers and mothers who hear me, beware, I implore you, of rearing your children in softness. For me, if I have committed such and such crimes, the cause of it is that in my youth I was always allowed to do as I pleased." ("*L'on m'a tou-jours laissé aller au gré de ma volonté.*")

From a child, he showed distinction in the arts of war; appeared for a time clad in all the warlike virtues. Enormously rich, in his own right as well as by marriage, he was eagerly welcomed to the standard of Charles the Dauphin, who was correspondingly poor. We shall see him at Orleans, riding beside the Maid, one of her devoted admirers; through all the period of his youth, his public acts shone bright and gallant as his own sword.

The second period of his life shows the artist, the seeker, the man of boundless ambitions. He aspired to be "*litterateur savant et artiste.*"[1] He had a passion for the beautiful, a passion for knowledge; for manuscripts, music, drama, science, especially that so-called science of the occult. When he traveled, he carried with him his valuable library, from which he would not be separated: carried also

[1] Gilles de Rais,

51

his two splendid organs, his chapel, his military household. He kept his own court of over two hundred mounted men, knights, squires, pages, all magnificently equipped and maintained at his expense. At two of his cities, Machecoul and Tiffanges, he maintained all the clergy of a cathedral and a collegiate church. dean, archdeacon, etc., etc., twenty-five to thirty persons, who (like the library) accompanied him on his travels, no less splendidly dressed than the knights and squires.

Many pages of a bulky memoir are devoted to the various ways in which Gilles squandered his princely fortune. Our concern is with his efforts to restore it, or rather to make another when it was gone.

In the course of his studies, he had not neglected the then-still-popular one of alchemy, and to this he turned when no more money was to be had. Gold, it appeared, could be made; if so, he was the man to make it. Workshops were set up at Tiffanges, perhaps in that gloomy donjon tower which alone remains today of all that Arabian Nights castle of splendor and luxury. Alchemists were summoned and wrought night and day, spurred on by promises and threats. Night and day they wrought; but no gold appeared. Fearing for their lives, they hinted at other and darker things that might be necessary, at other agencies which might produce the desired result If my lord would call in, for example, those who dealt in magic——?

Frantic in his quest, Gilles stopped at nothing. Necromancers were sent for, and came; they in turn summoned "spirits from the vasty deep" or elsewhere, who obediently appeared. Trembling, yet exultant, Gilles de Rais spoke to the demons, asking for knowledge, power and riches (*"science, puissance, et richesse"*), promising in return anything and everything except his life and his soul. The demons, naturally enough, made no reply to this one-sided offer. It is curious to read of the midnight scenes in that summer of 1439 when Gilles and his magician-friend Prelati, with their three attendants, tried to strike this bargain with the infernal powers. Torches, incense, pentacles, crucibles, etc., etc.; nothing was omitted. They adjured Satan, Belial, and Beelzebub to appear and "speak up"; adjured them, singularly enough, in the name of the

Holy Trinity, of the Blessed Virgin and all the saints. The demons remained mute; nor were they moved by sacrifices of dove, pigeon or kid. Finally, a demon called "Barron" made response: it appeared that what the fiends desired was human sacrifice: that without it no favors might be expected of them.

About this time the western provinces of France became afflicted with a terrible scourge. A monster, it was whispered, a murderous beast, *bête d'extermination,* was hiding in the woods, none knew where. Children began to disappear; youths and maidens too, all young and tender human creatures. They vanished, leaving no trace behind. At first the bereaved parents lamented as over some natural accident. The little one had strayed from home, had fallen into the river, had lost its way in the forest. The friends mourned with them, but were hardly surprised: it was not too strange for those wild days. But the thing spread. In the next village, two children had disappeared; in the next again, four. The creature, whatever it was, grew bolder, more ravenous. Terror seized the people; the whole countryside was in an agony of fear and suspense. Rumor

Holy Trinity, of the Blessed Virgin and all the saints. The demons remained mute; nor were they moved by sacrifices of dove, pigeon or kid. Finally, a demon called "Barron" made response: it appeared that what the fiends desired was human sacrifice: that without it no favors might be expected of them.

About this time the western provinces of France became afflicted with a terrible scourge. A monster, it was whispered, a murderous beast, *bête d'extermination*, was hiding in the woods, none knew where. Children began to disappear; youths and maidens too, all young and tender human creatures. They vanished, leaving no trace behind. At first the bereaved parents lamented as over some natural accident. The little one had strayed from home, had fallen into the river, had lost its way in the forest. The friends mourned with them, but were hardly surprised: it was not too strange for those wild days. But the thing spread. In the next village, two children had disappeared; in the next again, four. The creature, whatever it was, grew bolder, more ravenous. Terror seized the people; the whole countryside was in an agony of fear and suspense. Rumor

spread far and wide; the beast took shape as
a human monster; the *ogre* was evolved, *Cro-
quemitaine,* who devoured children as we eat
bread. A little while, and the monster was
localized. It was within such a circle that the
children were vanishing; near Tiffanges, near
Machecoul, the two fairy castles of the great
Seigneur Gilles de Rais. Slowly but surely the
net of suspicion was drawn, closer, closer yet.
The whispers spread, grew bolder, finally
broke into open speech. "The beast of extermination" was none other than the Marshal
of France, the companion of Dunois and La
Hire, and of the Maid herself, the great lord
and mighty prince, Gilles de Rais. Search was
made in the chambers of Machecoul, in the
gloomy vaults of Tiffanges. The bones of the
murdered children were found, here lying in
heaps on the floor, there hidden in the depths
of well or oubliette. It is not a tale to dwell
upon; it is enough to know that in a few years
over three hundred children and young people
had been foully and cruelly done to death.

In 1440 the matter reached the drowsy ear
of Public Justice. Gilles was formally arrested
(making no resistance, secure in his own

power), was tried, tortured, and after making full confession and expressing repentance for his crimes, was condemned to be burned; but, meeting more tender executioners than did the Maid of France, was strangled instead, and his body piously buried by "certain noble ladies."

Every French child of education knows something of the *"jeune et beau Dunois"*, every French child, educated or not, knows the story of Joan of Arc; Anglo-Saxon children may not invariably attain this knowledge, but they all know Gilles de Rais, though they never heard his name. Soon after his death, he passed into the realm of Legend, and under the title of Bluebeard he lives, and will live as long as there are children. Legend, that enchanting but inaccurate dame, gave him his seven wives; he had but one, and she survived him. His own name soon passed out of use. Even in the town of Nantes, where he met his death, the expiatory monument raised by Marie de Rais on the place of her father's torture was called *"le monument de Barbe-Bleue."*

So, strangely enough, it is the children who keep alive the memory of their slayer.

ing, was beaten off, and the beasts were brought back in safety to Domrémy, where the happy villagers received them with shouts of joy.

The English were not directly responsible for this raid. Orly was a free-lance, robbing and harrying on his own account; Vaudemont was Anglo-Burgundian at heart. None the less, people, here as everywhere, were beginning to feel that war and trouble had come with the English, and that there could be no lasting peace or quiet while they trod the soil of France.

Not long after this raid, about noon of a summer day, Joan of Arc was in her father's garden, which lay between the house and the little gray church. We do not know just what the girl was doing, whether gathering flowers for her pleasure, or herbs for household use, or simply dreaming away a leisure hour, as girls love to do. Suddenly "on her left hand, toward the church, she saw a great light, and had a vision of the archangel Michael, surrounded by other angels." [1]

[1] Lowell "Joan of Arc," p 28 N. B—Other authorities place the light on her *right* hand

Thus, briefly and simply, the marvelous story begins. Indeed, the beginning must needs be brief, since only Joan herself could tell of the vision, and she was always reticent about it. She would not, press her as they might, describe the appearance of the archangel. We must picture him for ourselves, and this, thanks to Guido Reni, we may easily do. The splendid young figure in the sky-blue corslet, his fair hair afloat about his lightning countenance as he raises his sword above the prostrate Dragon, is familiar to us all. We may, if you please, fancy him similarly attired in the little garden at Domrémy, but the lightning would be softened to a kindlier glow as he addressed the frightened child.

Michael, chief of the seven (some say eight) archangels, is mentioned five times in the Scriptures, always as fighting: his festival (September 29th) should be kept, one might think, with clash of swords instead of chime of bells. We read that he was the special protector of the Chosen People; that he was the messenger of peace and plenty, the leader of the heavenly host in war, the representative of the Church triumphant; that his name means

"God's power," or "who is like God." As late
as 1607, the red-velvet-covered buckler said to
have been carried by him in his war with Luci-
fer was shown in a church in Normandy, till
its exhibition was forbidden by the Bishop of
Avranches. On the promontory of Malea is
a chapel built to him; when the wind blows
from that quarter, the sailors call it the beat-
ing of St. Michael's wings, and in sailing past
they pray the saint to keep the great wings
folded till they have rounded the cape. Of St.
Michael's Mount in Cornwall, it is told that
whatever woman sits in the rocky seat known
as Michael's Chair, will rule her husband ever
after. For further light on St. Michael, see
Paradise Lost. It remained for a poet of our
own day, more lively than Miltonic, to fix him
in our minds with a new epithet:

"When Michael, the Irish archangel, stands,
The angel with the sword " [1]

Little Joan, trembling among her rose-
bushes, knew, we may imagine, none of these
things. She saw "Messire Saint Michel" as a
heavenly prince with his attending angels:

[1] W B Clarke "The Fighting Race."

"there was much light from every side," she said, "as was fitting." He spoke to her; bade her be a good girl, and go often to church. Then the vision faded.

Seven years later, answering her judges, she speaks thus of the matter: "When I was thirteen years old (or about thirteen) I had a Voice from God, to help me in my conduct. And the first time, I was in great fear."

We may well believe it. We can fancy the child, her eyes still dazzled with the heavenly light, the heavenly voice still in her ears, stealing back into the house, pale and trembling. She said no word to mother Isabel or sister Catherine of what had come to her; for many a day the matter was locked in her own faithful heart.

The vision came again. The archangel promised that St. Catherine and St. Margaret should come to give her further help and comfort, and soon after these heavenly visitants appeared. "Their heads were crowned with fair crowns," says Joan, "richly and preciously. To speak of this I have leave from the Lord. . . . Their voices were beautiful, gentle and sweet."

We are not told which of the six St. Catherines it was who came to Joan; whether the Alexandrian maiden martyred in 307, she of the wheel and the ring; or St. Catherine of Siena, who at Joan's birth had been dead but thirty years, who had herself seen visions and heard voices, and who by her own voice swayed kings and popes and won the hearts of all men to her; or whether it was one of the lesser lights of that starry name.

As to St. Margaret, there can be no doubt; she was the royal Atheling, queen and saint of Scotland, one of the gracious and noble figures of history. We may read to-day how, sailing across the narrow sea, bound on a visit to her mother's father, the King of Hungary (through whom she could claim kinship with St. Ursula and with St. Elizabeth of Hungary) her vessel was storm-driven up the Firth of Forth, to find shelter in the little bay still known as St. Margaret's Hope. (Close by was the Queen's Ferry, known to readers of Scott and Stevenson; to-day the monstrous Forth Bridge has buried both spots under tons of stone and iron.) Visitors were rare on that coast in the time of Malcolm III., especially ladies "of incomparable beauty." Word was hastily sent to the King hard by in his palace of Dunfermline, and he as hastily came down to see for himself; saw, loved, wooed and won, all in short space. History makes strange bedfellows; it is curious to think that Joan's saintly visitor was so early Queen of Scotland only by grace of Macbeth's dagger, which slew the gentle Duncan, her husband's father.

Joan knew St. Margaret well; there was a statue of her in the church of Domrémy. The gracious ladies spoke kindly to her: permitted her to embrace them; bade her, as St. Michael had bidden her, to be good, to pray, to attend church punctually.

The visions became more or less regular, appearing twice or thrice a week; Joan was obedient to them, did all they asked, partly no doubt through awe and reverence, but also because she felt from the first that a great thing had come to her. "The first time that I heard the Voice, I vowed to keep my maidenhood so long as God pleased."

If a great thing had come to her, one was demanded of her in return. The heavenly ladies, when they had told her their names, bade her "help the king of France." This was a strange thing. She, a poor peasant maiden, humble and obscure, with no knowledge save of household matters and of tending sheep and cattle; what had she to do with kings? Joan might well have asked herself this, but she did not ask the saints. She listened reverently and waited for further light upon her path. The light came very gradually; it was as if the ladies were gentling a wild bird, coming a little and still a little nearer, till they could touch, could caress it, could still the frightened panting of the tiny breast. Soon the girl came to love them dearly, so that when they left her she wept and longed to go with them. This went on for three years, Joan still keeping the matter wholly to herself. She did her work punctually and faithfully; drove the cattle, sewed, spun and wove. No one knew or guessed that anything strange had come into her life. It was seen that she grew graver, more inclined to religious exercises and to solitary musing, less and less ready to join the village frolics; but this was nothing specially remarkable in a pious French maiden of those days. It was a more serious matter that she should refuse an offer of marriage, a suitable offer from a responsible young man: her parents protested, but in vain. It was as if the suitor did not exist for her. In after years, when the folk of Domrémy were besieged with questions about Joan's childhood and girlhood, they racked their brains for significant memories, but found few or none. Thereupon my Lady Legend came kindly to their aid, and in an astonishingly short space of time a host of supernatural matters transpired. Some of the stories were very pretty; as that of the race in the river-meadows, the prize a nosegay, won by Joan, who ran so lightly that her feet seemed hardly to touch the ground. "Joan," cried one of the girls, "I see you flying close to the earth!" Presently, the race over, and Joan at the end of the meadow, "as it were rapt and distraught," she saw a youth beside her who said, "Joan, go home; your mother needs you!" Joan hastened home, only to be reproved by Dame Isabel for leaving her sheep.

"Did you not send for me?" asked the Maid. Assured of this, she turned meekly back, when there passed before her eyes a shining cloud, and from the cloud came a voice bidding her "change her course of life, and do marvelous deeds, for the King of Heaven had chosen her to aid the King of France. She must wear man's dress, take up arms, be a captain in the war, and all would be ordered by her advice."

Some historians accept, others reject this story: "I tell the tale that I heard told."

For several years—some say three, some five—the Maid kept these things in her heart. But now the Voices (she always called them so) became more explicit. She must "go into France."

(Here arise questions concerning the borders of Bar and Lorraine, which concern us little to-day, albeit volumes have been written about them. Domrémy was actually in France, but not in that part of it held by the Orleanists; Burgundy lay between, and several broad provinces held by the English: yet the people of Domrémy were French, every fibre of them, and not a heart in the village but was with Charles of Valois in his struggle to regain his father's crown.)

She must go to France, said the Voices,

because of the "great pity" that was there. She must save France, must save the king. Over and over again, this was repeated, till the words might have been found written on her heart, as "Calais" on Mary Tudor's.

It was the autumn of 1428, and "Orleans" was the word on all lips and in all hearts of Frenchmen. The English were encamped around the city, had invested it; the siege had begun. If Orleans fell, France fell with her. Clearer and clearer came the Voices. Not only France, but Orleans, Joan was bidden to save. This done, she must seek the Dauphin Charles, must lead him to Rheims and there see him crowned king. What she must do thereafter was not clear; the Voices rang confusedly. Something there was about driving the English from France. But now, now, *now*, she must be about the work in hand. She must go to Robert of Baudricourt at Vaucouleurs, and ask him for an escort to the Dauphin.

"I am a poor girl!" cried the Maid. "I have never sat a horse; how should I lead an army?"

Clearer and stronger day by day the Voices

67

reiterated their command. She must go, go, go to Vaucouleurs.

At last Joan could resist no longer. "The time went heavily with me, as with a woman in travail." She resolved to go "into France," though, she said, unless at God's bidding, she would rather be torn by wild horses than leave Domrémy.

About this time Jacques d'Arc had a dream, wherein he saw his daughter riding in company with armed men. He was both frightened and angry "If I knew of your sister's going," he said to his sons, Peter and John, "I would bid you drown her; if you refused, I would drown her myself."

While Joan is standing on the threshold, looking out wide-eyed into that new, strange world of war and bloodshed for which she must leave forever the small safe ways of home, let us try to form some idea of what she was going out for to see.

CHAPTER VI

THE EMPTY THRONE

Alez-vous en, alez, alez,
Soussi, Soing, et Mérencolie,
Me cuidez-vous toute ma vie
Gouverner, comme fait avez

Je vous promet que non ferez;
Raison aura sur vous maistrie:
Alez-vous en, alez, alez,
Soussi, Soing et Mérencolie

Se jamais plus vous retournez
Avecques vostre compaignie
Je pri à Dieu qu'il vous maudie
Et ce par qui vous revendrez:
Alez-vous en, alez, alez
                        —*Charles d'Orléans*

AT the funeral of Charles VI. of France
(November 11th, 1422) John, Duke
of Bedford, was the solitary mourner. Alone
he walked, the sword of state borne before
him as Regent of France; alone he knelt at the
requiem mass· an alien and a stranger. The
people of Paris looked on in silence; they had
nothing to say. "They wept," we are told

69

by a contemporary, "and not without cause, for they knew not whether for a long, long while they would have any king in France."

A few days before this, on October thirtieth, Charles the Dauphin had assumed the title of king, and at a high mass in the cathedral of Bourges had made his first royal communion. "The king of Bourges," those of the Anglo-Burgundian party called him; none of them thought he would ever be anything else. He was twenty years old at this time. We shall make his personal acquaintance later; our business now is with the country over which he assumed sovereignty.

Philip the Good, Duke of Burgundy, did not attend the funeral of his late master; he had no idea of yielding precedence to John of Bedford He sent chamberlains and excuses; was England's faithful ally, he protested, but was very busy at home.

The war meantime was going on as best it might. There were various risings in Charles's favor: in Paris itself, in Troyes, in Rheims; all put down with a strong hand. At Rheims, the superior of the Carmelite friars was accused of favoring the banished prince; he did not deny it, and declared stoutly, "Never was English king of France, and never shall be!" In Paris, several citizens were beheaded, and one woman burned; with little effect save on the sufferers themselves.

There was fighting in the field, too; here a skirmish, there an ambuscade, here again something that might pass for a battle. At Crevent-sur-Yonne, at Verneuil, the French (as we must now call Charles's followers) were defeated; at La Gravelle they were victorious. A pretty thing happened in connection with this last battle. In a castle hard by the field lived Anne de Laval, granddaughter of Bertrand du Guesclin. Hearing the clash of arms, seeing from her tower, it may be, French and English set in battle array, the lady sent for her twelve-year-old son, Andrew de Laval, and with trembling, yet eager hands, buckled round him the sword of the great Breton captain.

"God make thee as valiant," she said, "as he whose sword this was!" and sent him to the field. The boy did good service that day; was knighted on the field of battle, and lived to carry out, as marshal of France, the promise of his childhood.

Far north, perched like an eagle on a crag above the sea, stood *Mont St. Michel au peril de la mer,* the virgin fortress-abbey; a sacred spot even under the Druids; these many hundred years now one of the holy places of France, under special patronage of St. Michael, the archangel of Joan's vision. England greatly desired this coign of vantage; made overtures thereanent to the abbot, Robert Jolivet, who listened and finally promised to surrender the place to them. He went to Rouen to conclude the bargain. No sooner was he safely out of the abbey than the chapter of valiant monks elected one of their number, John Enault, vicar-general, shut and barred the gate (there was but one), raised the portcullis, and bade defiance to abbot and English. The latter found that the friendly churchman had exaggerated his own powers, and theirs. Surrounded by wide-spreading quicksands, its sheer walls buffeted day and night by the Atlantic surges, Mont St. Michel could be taken only by treachery, and the one traitor was now safely barred out. Aided by some valiant Norman warriors who chanced to be in the abbey on pilgrimage or other business, the monks of

St. Michael, worthy of their warlike patron, held their fortress for eight long years against all assaults, preserving it inviolate for their rightful king.

Far to southward, La Rochelle, "proud city of the waters," made like resistance to the invaders. The Rochellais knew the English of old. John Lackland had landed there when he came in 1214 to try to recover certain lands seized by Philip Augustus shortly before. It remained in English hands till 1224, when it was captured by Louis VIII.; was restored by treaty to the English in 1360; finally shook off the foreign yoke in Du Guesclin's time. Now it was one of the great maritime cities of France, its mariners sailing all seas, hardy and bold as Drake or Magellan.

On August 15th, 1427, an English fleet of one hundred and twenty sail appeared off the port, bringing troops for an invasion. La Rochelle promptly strengthened her defences, laid a heavy tax on herself to meet expenses, and sent out a fleet of armed privateers to meet the invaders, who, after some deliberation, withdrew without attempting to land.

Tired of this war of wasps—a sting, a

flight, a sting again—John of Bedford resolved to strike a decisive blow, one which should bring the wasps' nest down once and for all. The blow fell upon Orleans.

Royal Orleans (several kings were consecrated in its cathedral and lodged in its palaces) lies on the right bank of the Loire, one of the sacred cities of France. It had been besieged before, in 451, by Attila, the Hun of the period, who failed to gain entrance. Forty-odd years later, Clovis got possession of the city, and held there the first Council of France. Philip of Valois made it a separate duchy; Charles VI. gave it to his brother Louis, and the House of Orleans came into existence.

The city stretched along the river bank some nine hundred yards, and back to a depth of six hundred yards; was protected by a wall from twenty to thirty feet high, with parapet, machicolations, and twenty-four towers; and on all sides—except that of the river—by a ditch forty feet wide and twenty feet deep. The river was spanned by a bridge three hundred and fifty yards long, the centre resting on an island, its further end protected by a

small fortress called *Les Tourelles,* which in
its turn was covered by a strong earthwork
known as the *boulevard.*

Now, in the autumn of 1428, all eyes were
turned on the city, and on the ring of "bastilles"
(palisaded earthworks) surrounding it, com-
manding every approach. In these bastilles
and in the camps stretching beyond them on
every side, the English commanders were
gathered: Salisbury, Suffolk, Talbot, Scales,
Fastolf. Inside the city walls were Dunois, La
Hire, Xaintrailles, La Fayette—beside these
the citizens fought with desperate courage. On
both sides captains and soldiers girded themselves for a struggle which all felt must be a
decisive one. Assault on one side, sortie on
the other, began and continued briskly. Salisbury with his curious copper cannon (throwing
stone balls of one hundred and fifty pounds'
weight a distance of seven hundred yards) battered the walls and rained shot into the city:
the besieged replied with boiling oil, lime, and
the like, with which the women of Orleans kept
them supplied. The fight raged with greatest
violence round the Tourelles, which English
and French were equally determined to take

and to keep. After being battered almost to pieces, it was finally captured by the besiegers, but at terrible cost. On the eighth day of the siege (October) Salisbury, standing by an embrasure in one of its towers, was struck on the head by a stone ball from a French cannon, and died soon after. This was a heavy loss to the English. On the other hand, Sir John Fastolf, convoying provisions for the English, completely routed a party of French, who sallied out to intercept him. Lent was near, and prudent Sir John had procured a large supply of salt herrings; these, scattered over the field in every direction, gave the skirmish its name, the Battle of the Herrings. Most of the provender was brought safely into camp, rejoicing greatly the hearts of the English. But the city managed to get victualed too. One day six hundred pigs were driven in, spite of cannon and mortar; another day two hundred, and forty beeves; but the day after they lost five hundred head of cattle and "the famous light field-piece of that master gunner, Jean the Lorrainer."[1] A merry wag, this John of Lorraine: his jests flew as fast as his balls. Now and

[1] A Lang, "Maid of France," p 63.

then he would drop beside his gun, and be carried off apparently dead. Shouts of joy would go up from the English: in the midst of which, John would "bob up serenely" bowing and smiling, and would go to work again.

So, back and forth, the tide ebbed and flowed, while the winter dragged on. A leisurely, almost a cheerful siege; Andrew Lang thinks the fighting was "not much more serious than the combats with apples and cheeses, in the pleasant land of Torelore, as described in the old romance of *Aucassin and Nicolete*."[1] He quotes the Monk of Dunfermline, "a mysterious Scots chronicler,"[1] as saying that the English camp was like a great fair, with booths for the sale of all sorts of commodities, and with sunk ways leading from one fort to another.

All this time, under cover of the desultory shooting, the English were drawing the ring of fortifications closer and closer yet about the city. In the gloomy days of February, the citizens began to lose heart. No more provisions came in. Dunois, now their leader, a natural son of Louis of Orleans, and the brav-

[1] Andrew Lang. "Maid of France," p 63

est heart in France save one, was wounded. People began to leave the city, stealthily, under cover of night. The bishop left; Clermont, who had lost the Battle of the Herrings, stole away, taking two thousand men with him: the admiral and chancellor of France "thought it would be a pity to have the great officers of the crown taken by the English, and went too." [1]

Dunois sent La Hire to the Dauphin at Chinon, begging for men, money, food. The receiver-general, he was told, had not four crowns in his chest. Charles kept the messenger to dinner, and regaled him with a fowl and a sheep's tail. La Hire returning empty-handed, Dunois in desperation sent to Philip of Burgundy, begging him to take the city under his protection. Philip of Burgundy, always distracted between his hatred of the Dauphin and his fear of the growing power of the English, sent a message asking the Duke of Bedford to raise the siege; but this John of Bedford was in nowise minded to do.

"We are not here to champ the morsels for Burgundy to swallow!" said one of his advisers.

[1] Michelet. "Histoire de France."

"Nay! nay!" assented Duke John. "We will not beat the bushes for another to take the birds!"

High words ensued, and Philip withdrew his men from the siege. John cared little, had plenty without them. English and French, all thought the city was doomed: through all France men sighed and wept over its approaching fall; and across the Channel, in the White Tower, the captive lord of Orleans wept with them, and tuned his harp to songs of grief.

> L'un ou l'autre desconfira
> De mon cueur et Mérencolie;
> Auquel que fortune s'alye,
> L'autre "je me rens" lui dira
>
> D'estre juge me suffira
> Pour mettre fin en leur folye;
> L'un ou l'autre desconfira
> De mon cueur et Mérencolie.
>
> Dieu scet comment mon cueur rira
> Se gaigne, menant chière lye,
> Contre ceste saison jolye,
> On verra comment en yra
> L'un ou l'autre desconfira
> —*Charles d'Orléans*

April was come, and the end seemed near, when whispers began to creep about. A bird of the air carried the matter, a wind of the forest breathed it. Help was coming. A marvel had come to light: a holy Maid (or an accursed witch: it depended on which camp you were in!) had arisen, had visited the Dauphin at Chinon: was coming to rescue Orleans from its besiegers. Like wildfire the rumor spread. Brave Dunois listened, and his heart beat faster, recalling the prophecy. "France lost by a woman shall be saved by a woman!" Could it be? Was Heaven, after all, on the side of France?

The English listened too; not the King, for he was, we will hope, sleeping comfortably in his cradle at Windsor; but John of Bedford in Paris (not in that haunted Palace of St. Paul, but in the more cheerful one of Les Tourelles across the way); and before Orleans, his lieutenants, Suffolk, Talbot, Scales, and the rest. These gentlemen were amused. The Dauphin must be fallen low indeed to avail himself of such aid. They made merry in the English camp, and laugh and jest went round at the expense of their sorry adversary, clinging to the red petticoat of a peasant girl (for so rumor described her) for succor and relief.

Suddenly, one April day, the laughter ceased. A letter was brought into the camp: a message brief and sharp as a sword-thrust greeted the astonished captains.

"*Jesu Maria*," thus it began:

"King of England, account to the King of Heaven for His blood royal. Give up to the Maid the keys of all the good towns you have taken by force. She is come from God to avenge the blood royal, and quite ready to make peace, if you will render proper account. If you do not so, I am a war-chief; in whatsoever place I shall fall in with your folk in France, if they be not willing to obey, I shall make them get thence, whether they will or not; and if they be willing to obey, I will receive them to mercy. . . . The Maid cometh from the King of Heaven as His representative, to thrust you out of France; she doth promise and certify you that she will make therein such mighty *haha* (great tumult), that for a thousand years hitherto in France was never the like. . . . Duke of Bedford, who call yourself regent of France, the Maid doth pray you and request you not to bring destruction on yourself; if you do not justice towards her, she will do the finest deed ever done in Christendom.

"Writ on Tuesday in the great week" (Easter week, March, 1429). Subscribed: *"Hearken to the news from God and the Maid."* [1]

The hour was come, and the Maid. Let us go back a little, and see the manner of her coming.

---

[1] Guizot. "History of France."

CHAPTER VII

VAUCOULEURS AND CHINON

"GO to Vaucouleurs!" the Voices had said: "go to Robert of Baudricourt, and bid him send thee to the Dauphin!" Again and yet again, "Go!"

Vaucouleurs, the "valley of color," is a little walled town on the Meuse, some thirteen miles from Domrémy. Its narrow streets climb a steep hill to the castle, perched on its rock like an eagle's nest. In this castle, holding the town partly for the Dauphin, but chiefly for himself, lived Robert of Baudricourt; a robber captain, neither more nor less. A step beyond the highwayman, since he had married a rich and noble widow, and had lived handsomely in (and on) Vaucouleurs for some twelve years; but still little more civilized than the band of rude and brutal soldiers under his command. It was from this man that the Maid was bidden to seek aid in her mission

She bethought her of a kinsman, Durand Laxart (or Lassois) living at Little Burey, a village near Vaucouleurs; asked and obtained leave of her parents to visit him. This was in May, 1428. She opened her mind to her "uncle" (by courtesy: he was really only a cousin by marriage) and impressed him so much that he consented to bring her before the lord of the castle.

Baudricourt looked at the comely peasant maid in her red stuff dress, probably with some interest at first; when she quietly informed him that God had bidden her to save France, and had sent her to him for help in the task, his interest changed to amused impatience. At first he laughed; but when he was called upon in God's name to send a message to the Dauphin his mood changed.

"Let him guard himself well," the message ran, "and not offer battle to his foes, for the Lord will give him succor by mid-Lent."

Now Lent was to fall in March of the coming year.

"By God's will," the Maid added, "I myself will lead the Dauphin to be crowned."

This was too much for the lord of Vaucouleurs. Turning to Laxart, he said, "Give the wench a sound whipping and send her home!" and so dismissed the pair.

Joan made no resistance; went back to Domrémy and bided her time. We are to suppose that through the summer of 1428 she plied her faithful tasks at home, listening to her Voices, strengthening her purpose steadily in the quiet of her resolute heart. In October came the news that Orleans was besieged; and now once more the Voices grew urgent, imperative; yet again she must go to Vaucouleurs, yet again demand help of Robert of Baudricourt. This time the way was made easy for her. The wife of Durand Laxart was about to have a child, and needed help. There were no trained nurses then in the Meuse valley or anywhere else; it was the simple and natural thing for Joan to offer her services, and for the kinsfolk to accept them. January, 1489, found her domiciled in the Laxart household, caring for the mother and the new-born child in her own careful, competent way.

One day she told her kinsman that she must see My Lord of Baudricourt once more, and besought him to bear her company. He de-

murred; they had got little good of the first
visit, he reminded her.

"Do you not know," asked the girl, "the
saying that France is to be made desolate by
a woman and restored by a Maid?" and added
that she must go "into France" and lead the
Dauphin to Rheims for his coronation. Laxart
had heard the prophecy; most people knew it,
in the Meuse valley and elsewhere. He
yielded, and once more the peasant man and
maid made their way up the climbing street
and appeared before the lord of the castle.
We do not know that the second interview
prospered much better than the first. Laxart
says that Baudricourt bade him "more than
once" to box the girl's ears and send her home
to her father; but this time Joan did not go
home. After spending several weeks with her
cousin's family, she went to stay with a family
named Royer, where she helped in the house-
work, and "won the heart of her hostess by
her gentle ways, her skill in sewing, and her
earnest faith."[1]

This must have been a season of anguish
for the Maid. France was dying: they thought

[1] Lang "Maid of France," p 65

it then as they thought it in 1918: she alone
could save her country, and no man would give
her aid, would even listen to her. Perhaps at no
time—save at the last—is the heroic quality
of the Maid more clearly shown than in the
meagre record of these weeks of waiting.
How should she sit to spin, with saints and
angels calling in her ear? How should she
ply her needle, when the sword was waiting
for her hand? But the needle flew swiftly, the
spindle whirled diligently, and day and night
her prayers went up to God. People recalled
afterward how often they had seen her in the
church of St. Mary on the hill above the town,
kneeling in rapt devotion, her face now bowed
in her hands, now lifted in passionate appeal.
Courage, Joan! the time is near, and help is
coming.

It was in February, 1429, that the first
gleam of encouragement came to her. She met
in the street a young man-at-arms named Jean
de Metz, often called, from the name of his
estate, Jean de Novelonpont. He had heard
of her: probably by this time everyone in
Vaucouleurs knew of her and her mission.
Seeing her in her red peasant-dress, he stopped

and said, "*Ma mie,* what are you doing here?
Must the King be walked out of his kingdom,
and must we all be English?"

Joan looked at him with her clear dark eyes.

"I am come," she answered, "to a Royal
town to ask Robert de Baudricourt to lead me
to the King. But Baudricourt cares nothing
for me and for what I say; none the less I
must be with the King by mid-Lent, if I wear
my legs down to the knees. No man in the
world—kings, nor dukes, nor the daughter of
the Scottish king—can recover the kingdom of
France, nor hath our king any succor save
from myself, though I would liefer be sewing
beside my poor mother. For this deed is not
convenient to my station. Yet go I must; and
this deed I must do, because my Lord so
wills it."

"And who is your Lord?" asked Jean de
Metz: and the Maid replied,

"My Lord is God!" [1]

Our hearts thrill to-day as we read the
words; think how they fell on the ear of the
young soldier there in the village street that
winter day! He needed no voice of saint or

[1] Trans Andrew Lang.

angel: this simple maiden's voice was enough. He held out his hand.

"Then I, Jean, swear to you, Maid, my hand in your hands, that I, God helping me, will lead you to the King, and I ask when you will go?"

"Better to-day than to-morrow: better to-morrow than later!" [1] was the reply.

From that day forth, Jean de Metz was Joan's faithful friend and helper.

What did she mean about help from Scotland? Why, a year before the Dauphin had sent Alain Chartier the poet to Scotland to beg help of the ancient ally of France. Help was promised; six thousand men, to arrive before Whitsuntide; to form moreover a body-guard for the little Princess of Scotland, another Margaret, who was to marry little Louis, son of the Dauphin. Joan had heard rumors of all this; but what was a baby princess three hundred leagues away? She, the Maid, was on the spot.

"Go boldly on!" said the Voices. "When you are with the King, he will have a sure sign to persuade him to believe and trust you."

[1] Trans Andrew Lang

As it fell out, the little princess did not come till seven years later: the six thousand men never came at all.

At last Joan had a friend who could give real help. A few days more and she had two: Bertrand of Poulangy, another young soldier, heard and believed her story, and took his stand beside her and Jean de Metz. The three together renewed the attack on Robert de Baudricourt, this time with more success. Apparently this was not so simple a case as had appeared: whipping, ear-boxing, no longer seemed adequate. What to do? Puzzled and annoyed, Baudricourt bethought him of the spiritual arm. After all, what more simple than to find out whether this counsel was of God or the devil? One evening, we are told, he entered the humble dwelling of the Royers, accompanied by the parish priest. The latter, assuming his stole, addressed the Maid in solemn tones.

"If thou be a thing of evil," he said, "begone from us! If a thing of good, approach us!"

Joan had knelt when the good father put on his garb of office; now, still on her knees, slowly and painfully (but with head held high, we may fancy) she made her way forward to where the priest stood. She was not pleased. It was ill-done of Father Fournier, she said afterward; had he not heard her fully in confession? It may be—who knows?—that the *curé* took this way to convince the lord of Baudricourt of her truth and virtue: be it as it may, Robert de Baudricourt no longer laughed at the peasant girl in her red dress; but still he was not ready to help her, and she could wait no longer. She resolved to walk to Chinon, where the Dauphin was; she borrowed clothes from her cousin Laxart, now for the first time assuming male attire; and so took her way to the shrine of St. Nicholas, on the road to France.

Now it took a horseman eleven days to ride from Vaucouleurs to Chinon; Joan soon realized that to make the journey on foot would be wasting precious time; she returned to Vaucouleurs, saddened, but no whit discouraged. About this time the Duke of Lorraine heard of the Maid who saw visions and heard voices. Being old and infirm and more interested in his own ailments than in those of the kingdom, he sent for Joan as we send for a new doctor who has cured our neighbor; sent moreover a letter of safe conduct, an important thing in those days. Here was Opportunity knocking at the door! A horse was bought— it is not clear by whom—and Joan and the faithful "uncle," accompanied by Jean de Metz, rode off in high hopes to Nancy, seventy miles away. Alas! here again disappointment awaited her. The Duke related his symptoms and asked for advice; hinted that perhaps a little miracle, even, might be performed? Such things had been done by holy maids before now! Joan told him briefly that she knew nought of these matters. Let him lend her his son-in-law, and men to lead her into France, and she would pray for his health. The son-in-law was René of Anjou, later known as the patron of minstrels and poets; an interesting if a somewhat fantastic figure. At this time his duchy of Bar was being so harried by French and English indiscriminately that he might well cry, "A plague of both your houses!" Certainly he gave no help to Joan. The old Duke of Lorraine gave her a black horse, some say, and a small sum of money;

and so a second time, she returned to Vaucouleurs.

But now the town itself was roused. Every one by this time knew the Maid and had heard of her mission. Since that visit of the *curé* they held her in reverence; moreover, the news from Orleans grew worse and worse. The fall of the city was looked for any day, and with it would fall the kingdom. Since all else had failed, why not let the Maid prove her Voices to be of God?

We know not what pressure, apart from Joan's own burning words (for she never ceased her appeals), was brought to bear on Robert de Baudricourt. At last, and most reluctantly, he yielded; gave consent that Joan should seek the Dauphin at Chinon; gave her even, it would seem, a letter to the prince, testifying some belief in her supernatural powers. The good people of Vaucouleurs put together their pennies and bought a suit of clothes for her: man's clothes, befitting one who was undertaking a man's work. Thus equipped, on the twelfth of February, 1429, Joan of Arc rode out of Vaucouleurs to save France. Beside her, on either side, rode her two faithful squires, Jean de Metz and Bertrand de Poulangy, with their servants; two more men, "Richard the Archer," and Colet de Vienne, a king's messenger, joined the little band; in all six rode out of the Gate of France. At the gate, Robert de Baudricourt, moved for once, we may hope, out of his boisterous sardonic humor, gave the Maid a sword; and as the adventurers passed on, he cried after them: *"Allez! et vienne que pourra!"* ("Go! and come what come may!")

What awaited the Maid in "white Chinon by the blue Vienne?" Let us see!

Pantagruel suggests that the city of the Plantagenets was founded by Cain, and named for him, but this theory is more literary than accurate. A strong little city, Chinon, from the days when Fulk Nerra, the Black Falcon, rode on his wild raids and built his crescent line of fortresses from Anjou to Amboise, cutting the "monstrous cantle" of Touraine from the domains of Blois. A fierce little city, looking down on furious quarrels of Angevin princes, French and so-called English. Here died Henry II. of England, men said of a broken heart, muttering, "Shame, shame,

on a conquered king!" Here came Richard
Yea-and-Nay to look on his father's body,
which men said streamed blood as he approached it. Here John Lackland lived for a
while with his French wife, no more beloved
than he was elsewhere. Here, on Midsummer
Eve, 1305, Philip Augustus entered victorious,
and soon after English rule in France came
to an end for the time. Here, in 1309, Jacques
de Molay, Grand Master of the Knights
Templar, was tried by a council of cardinals,
set on by Charles of Valois, first of the name,
who was in sore need of money and coveted
the rich possessions of the great order.
Master and many knights were burned (in
Paris, not in the place of their trial) and the
Order was dissolved.

More important, it may be, in the long
sequence of human events, than any of these
matters, here in 1483, was born *Maître*
François Rabelais, whose statue still looks
kindly down on the city of his love. "*Ville
insigne, ville noble, ville antique, voire première
du monde,*"[1] he calls it. He remains king of

[1] Famous city, noble city, ancient city, verily first of
earth

95

it, however many crowned or uncrowned puppets may have flaunted it there by the blue Vienne.

In this year 1429, Charles the Dauphin was holding in Chinon his shadowy court. This deplorable prince, a king of shreds and patches, if ever one lived, was now twenty-seven years old, and had never done anything in particular except to pursue pleasure and to escape danger. Accounts differ as to his personal appearance. Monstrelêt, his contemporary, calls him "a handsome prince, and handsome in speech with all persons, and compassionate toward poor folk"; but is constrained to add "he did not readily put on his harness, and he had no heart for war if he could do without it." Another chronicler gives a less favorable account of his appearance. "He was very ugly, with small gray wandering eyes; his nose was thick and bulbous, his legs bony and bandy; his thighs emaciated, with enormous knock-knees." Yet another dwells on his physical advantages, and his kindness of manner, which won the favor of the people. It does not greatly matter now what he looked like. When a flame springs up and lights the sky, we do not scrutinize the match that struck out the spark.

There he was at Chinon, surrounded by courtiers and favorites (chief among them La Trémoille, "the evil genius of king and country") amusing himself as best he might.

"Never a king lost his kingdom so gaily!" said La Hire. One of Joan's biographers [1] says of him: "Weak in body and mind, idle, lazy, luxurious, and cowardly, he was naturally the puppet of his worst courtiers, and the despair of those who hoped for reform"; and he quotes the burning words addressed by Juvenal des Ursins to his master, when king of France: "How many times have poor human creatures come to you to bewail the grievous extortion practiced upon them! Alas, well might they cry, 'Why sleepest thou, O Lord!' But they could arouse neither you nor those about you."

Charles was not always gay: he was subject to fits of deep depression, when he despaired of crown and kingdom, questioning even his right to either. Son of a mad father and a bad mother, was he indeed the rightful heir? In these moods he would leave his parasite

[1] Lowell "Joan of Arc," p 55

court and weep and pray apart. A pitiable creature, altogether.

Word was brought to Charles on a day that a young maid was at the gate, asking to see him; a maid in man's attire, riding astride a horse and five men-at-arms with her. Here was a strange matter! Charles had heard nothing of maids or missions. While he debated the matter with La Trémoille (to whom, by the way, he had pledged Chinon for whatever it would bring) and the rest, came a letter from the Maid herself, dictated by her and sent on before, but delayed or neglected till now. She asked permission to enter his town of Chinon, for she had ridden one hundred and fifty leagues to tell him "things useful to him and known to her." [1] She would recognize him, she said, among all others.

Charles was puzzled: the courtiers shook their heads. Suppose this were a witch! For the Dauphin to receive a witch would be at once dangerous and discreditable. Let the young woman be examined, to find out whether, if she were really inspired, her inspiration were of heaven or of hell. Accordingly "certain

[1] Lang. "Maid of France," p 76

98

clerks and priests, men expert in discerning good spirits from bad," [1] visited Joan in the humble inn where she waited, and questioned her closely. She answered briefly; she could not speak freely save to the Dauphin alone. She had been sent to relieve Orleans and lead the prince to Rheims, there to be crowned king. This was all she had to say: but her simple faith, her transparent purity, so impressed the examiners, that they made a favorable report. There was no harm in the Maid, and since she professed to be the bearer of a divine message, it would be well for the Dauphin to receive her. Very reluctantly, Charles consented, and finally, one evening, a message summoned Joan to the castle.

[1] Lowell "Joan of Arc," p 57

CHAPTER VIII

RECOGNITION

Sera-elle point jamais trouvée
Celle qui ayme Louyaulté?
Eet qui a ferme voulenté
Sans avoir legière pensée

Il convient qu'elle soi criée
Pour en savoir la verité
Sera-elle point jamais trouvée
Celle qui ayme Louyaulté?

Je croy bien qu'elle est deffiée
Des aliéz de Faulceté,
Dont il y a si grant planté
Que de paour elle s'est mussiée
Sera-elle point jamais trouvée?
　　　　　　—Charles d'Orleans

I T was morning of March 6th, 1429, when
Joan rode out between her two faithful
squires to seek the Dauphin. Gladly she rode,
her eyes fixed on those white towers of Chinon
where her mission was to be accepted, where
she was to consecrate herself anew to the re-
demption of France. She felt no shadow of
doubt; she never felt any, till her true work

was done; yet, the old chronicles say, danger threatened her here at the outset. A band of outlaws, hearing of her approach, prepared an ambuscade, thinking to take the Maid and hold her for ransom. There they crouched in the woods hard by Chinon town, waiting; there they saw the little cavalcade draw near; the dark slender girl in her man's dress, the men-at-arms on either side; there they remained motionless, never stirring hand or foot, till the riders passed out of sight. Is it a true tale? If so, was it a miracle, as people thought then, the robbers held with invisible bonds, unable to stir hand or foot? Or was it—still greater marvel, perhaps—just the power of that up-lifted look, the white radiance of that face under the steel cap, which turned the men's hearts from evil thoughts to good?

Another tale is vouched for by eyewitnesses: how as the Maid rode over the bridge toward the city, a certain man-at-arms spoke to her in coarse and insulting language.

"Alas!" said Joan; "thou blasphemest thy God, and art so near thy death!"

He was drowned shortly after, whether by accident or by his own act, seems uncertain.

So the Maid came to Chinon, and after some further delay, was admitted, on the evening of March 29th, to the presence of the Dauphin. Chinon Castle is in ruins to-day. Of the great hall on the first story nothing remains save part of the wall and the great fireplace of carved stone; yet even these are hardly needed to call up the scene that March evening. We can see the fire crackling under the fine chimney-piece, the dozens of torches flinging their fitful glare about the great hall where some three hundred knights were gathered. They were standing in knots here and there, whispering together, waiting, some hopefully, some scornfully, for this importunate visitor, the peasant girl of Domrémy. In one of these knots stood Charles of Valois, far less splendidly dressed than some of his followers. He made no sign when Joan entered the hall, led by the high steward, Louis of Bourbon, Count of Vendôme: but his eyes, all eyes in that hall, were fixed curiously on the slender figure clad in black and gray, which advanced modestly yet boldly.

Joan of Arc was now seventeen years old: tall and well made. Guy de Laval wrote of her to his mother: "She seems a thing all divine, *de son faict,* and to see her and hear her." Others call her "beautiful in face and figure," her countenance glad and smiling.

> "Elle est plaisante en faite et dite,
> Belle et blanche comme la rose,"

says the old mystery play of the siege of Orleans.

Andrew Lang, the most sympathetic of her English biographers,[1] writes thus of her appearance:

"Her hair was black, cut short like a soldier's; as to her eyes and features, having no information, we may conceive of them as we please. Probably she had grey eyes, and a clear pale colour under the tan of sun and wind. She was so tall that she could wear a man's clothes, those, for example, of Durand Lassois."

There is no authentic likeness of the Maid; she never sat for her portrait; yet who is there that cannot picture to himself that slender figure, in the black *pourpoint,* with the short

[1] N B—He was a Scot!

gray cloak thrown back over her shoulder, coming forward to meet and greet the Prince to whom she was to give a kingdom, receiving in return a felon's grave?

Accounts vary as to the scene that followed Some chroniclers say that Joan asked that "she should not be deceived, but be shown plainly him to whom she must speak"; others assert that Charles turned aside at her approach, effacing himself, as it were, behind some of his followers. However it was, Joan showed no hesitation, but went directly up to the Prince and made obeisance humbly.

"Gentle Dauphin," she said, "I am called Joan the Maid. The King of Heaven sendeth you word by me that you shall be anointed and crowned in the city of Rheims, and shall be lieutenant of the King of Heaven, who is King of France. It is God's pleasure that our enemies, the English, should depart to their own country; if they depart not, evil will come to them, and the kingdom is sure to continue yours."

Charles listened, impressed but not yet convinced. He talked with her a little, and sent her back to her lodging (in a tower of the castle this time, in charge of "one William Bellier, an officer of the castle, and his wife, a matron of character and piety" [1]) without making any definite answer. This was hard for the Maid to bear; she knew there was no time to lose; yet she went patiently; she was used to waiting, used to rebuffs. There in her tower lodging, many visitors came to her: churchmen, with searching questions as to her orthodoxy; captains, no less keen in inquiry as to her knowledge of arms: finally, "certain noble dames," deputed by the Dauphin, to determine whether she were pure virgin or no. Doubtless these many persons came in many moods; they all left in one; the Maid was a good Maid, gentle and simple: there was no harm in her. Again and again she sought audience of the Dauphin. She could do nothing with a printed page, but the heart of a man, especially of this man, was easy reading for her.

"Gentle Dauphin," she said to him one day, "why do you not believe me? I say unto you that God hath compassion on you, your kingdom, and your people; St. Louis and Charle-

[1] Lowell. "Joan of Arc," p. 57.

magne are kneeling before Him, making prayer
for you, and I will say unto you, so please
you, a thing which will give you to understand
that you ought to believe me." [1]

One day, after mass, Charles led her into
a chamber apart, where were only La Trémoïlle and one other. He was in one of his
dark moods, his mind full of doubts and fears.
Was he after all the rightful heir? In his
closet that morning, he had prayed that if the
kingdom were justly his, God might be pleased
to defend it for him; if not, that he might
find refuge in Scotland or in Spain. Joan, we
may fancy, read all this in his face that day
in the castle chamber. Taking him aside, she
spoke long and earnestly.

"What she said to him there is none who
knows," wrote Alain Chartier the poet soon
after, "but it is quite certain that he was all
radiant with joy thereat as at a revelation from
the Holy Spirit."

Well he might be! on the authority of her
Voices, "on behalf of her Lord," the Maid
declared him true heir of France, and son of

the king." From that moment we may perhaps date the belief of Charles in her mission. One other, I said, besides Charles and La Trémoille, was present at the interview. This was the young Duke of Alençon, son-in-law of Charles of Orleans. He was then twenty years of age, as gallant and careless a lad as might be. At fifteen he had been taken prisoner in battle: was ransomed two years later, spite of his refusal to acknowledge Henry VI. King of France; had since then been living on his estate, amusing himself and taking little thought of the distracted country. He was shooting quails one day when word came of a mysterious Maid who had appeared before the King, claiming to be sent by God to drive out the English, and raise the siege of Orleans. Here, for once, was something interesting in these tiresome squabbles of Burgundian and Armagnac; something, it might be, more exciting than quail-shooting. He took horse and rode to Chinon; sought his cousin Charles, and found him deep in talk with the Maid herself.

"Who is this?" asked Joan.

"It is the Duke of Alençon," replied the Dauphin.

She turned to Alençon with her own simple grace.

"You are very welcome," she said. "The more princes of the blood that are here together, the better."

Alençon, warm and chivalrous by nature, felt none of the doubts which beset the Dauphin; he was charmed with the Maid, and she with him: it was friendship at first sight, and "the gentle duke," as she called him, became her sworn brother in arms.

Charles was now inclined to take Joan and her mission seriously, spite of the indifference (later to develop into bitter hostility) of La Trémoille. She had fired the despondent captains with hope of saving Orleans; had won the hearts of the court ladies, had satisfied the confessors of her orthodoxy; last and most important, she had performed what seemed to him a miracle in reading his thoughts. But nothing must be done hastily. In so important a matter, every authority must be consulted; it must be established beyond peradventure that this Maid was of God and not of Satan.

Paris was inaccessible, held by John of Bedford for his baby King: but at Poitiers was a University with many wise and holy men; was also a court or parliament of sorts, where law might be demonstrated if not enforced by learned lawyers and jurists. At Poitiers, if anywhere in Charles's pasteboard realm, the question might be decided: to Poitiers Joan should go.

Fifty miles: two days' ride, and Orleans in the death-struggle!

"To Poitiers?" cried the Maid. "In God's name I know I shall have trouble enough; but let us be going!"

She had had already trouble enough, more than enough, with lawyers and priests. She saw no sense in them. They droned on and on, splitting hairs, piling question on argument, when all she asked was a small company of men-at-arms; when her time was so short; when the Voices bade her go, go, go to save the city!

Small wonder if she lost patience now and then in the days that followed at Poitiers. They compassed her about on every side, Professors of Theology and of Law.

"What brought you to the King?" asked one.
She answered proudly, "A Voice came to me
while I was herding my flock, and told me that
God had great pity on the people of France,
and that I must go into France."

"If God wishes to deliver France," said
another, "He does not need men-at-arms."

"In God's name," said the Maid, "the men-
at-arms will fight, and God will give the
victory."

"What language does the Voice speak?"

This questioner, a Carmelite friar, spoke the
dialect of Limoges, his native province, and
Joan answered briefly:

"A better one than yours!"

"Do you believe in God?" the friar persisted.

"More firmly than you do!"

Joan then foretold the future as she saw it.
She would summon the English and, they refusing to submit, would force them to raise the
siege of Orleans After this the Dauphin
would be crowned at Rheims; Paris would
rally to his standard; finally, the Duke of
Orleans would return from England. All these
things happened, but only the first two were

seen by Joan's mortal eyes. Her time was short, indeed.

For six weeks now she had been examined, by priest and clerk, jurist and soldier, noble ladies and village matrons: and like her great Exemplar, no harm had been found in her. She had, it was true, given no "sign," but this she promised to do before Orleans, for so God commanded her. In God's name, therefore, she was bidden to proceed on her mission; was sent to Tours, thence to proceed, when suitably armed and equipped, to Orleans.

It is pleasant to read of a little interlude during this time of waiting: a visit made by Joan at St. Florent, the castle of the duke of Alençon. The mother and wife of the duke received her with open arms, and "God knows," says the family chronicler, "the cheer they made her during the three or four days she spent in the place."

The young Duchess was Joan of Orleans, daughter of the captive poet-duke: it was her own city that this wondrous Maid was come to save. A girl herself, generous, ardent, small wonder that she opened her arms. She confided to Joan her fears for her soldier-husband. He had been taken once by the English, had been absent several years: it had been bitter hard to raise the money for his ransom.

"Have no fear, my lady!" said the Maid. "I will bring him safe back to you, as well as he now is, or even better."

One would fain linger a little over this visit. There were so few pleasures for Joan, so little of all that girlhood commonly takes as its bright, unquestionable right. I like to think of the two girls together: the duchess probably in *huque* and *hennin* (whereof more anon), the Maid in the page's dress which she wore when not in armor. She loved bright colors and pretty things, as well as the other girl. She was only seventeen, "fair and white as the white rose." God help thee, sweet Maid!

The days in Tours were brief and happy for Joan. She was accepted: she had started on her way; she could well wait, watching and praying, while her suit of white armor was made. Andrew Lang tells us that "the armour included a helmet, which covered the head to its junction with the neck, while a shallow cup of steel protected the chin, moving on the same hinge as the *salade*—a screen of steel which in battle was drawn down over the face to meet the chin-plate, and, when no danger was apprehended, was turned back, leaving the face visible. A neck-piece or gorget of five overlapping steel plates covered the chest as far as the breastbone, where it ended in a point, above the steel corslet, which itself apparently was clasped in front, down the centre, ending at the waist. The hip joints were guarded by a band, consisting of three overlapping plates of steel; below this, over each thigh, was a kind of skirt of steel, open in the centre for freedom in riding. There were strong thick shoulderplates; yet one of these was pierced through and through by an arrow or crossbow bolt, at close quarters, when Jeanne was mounting a scaling ladder in the attack on the English fort at the bridge-head of Orleans. The steel sleeves had plates with covered hinges to guard the elbows; there were steel gauntlets, thigh-pieces, knee-joints, greaves, and steel shoes. The horse, a heavy-weight-carrier, had his chamfron of steel, and the saddle rose high at the pommel and behind the back. A *hucque*, or cloak of cloth of gold, velvet, or other rich material, was worn over the armour. For six days continuously Jeanne bore this weight of steel, it is said, probably in the campaign of Jargeau and Pathay. Her exploits were wrought, and she received her wounds, while she was leading assaults on fortified places, standard in hand."

No sword was made for Joan at Tours; her sword was elsewhere. Hear her tell about it!

"While I was at Tours or Chinon, I sent to seek for a sword in the church of St. Catherine of Fierbois, behind the altar; and presently it was found, all rusty."

Asked how she knew that the sword was there, she said: "It was a rusty sword in the earth, with five crosses on it, and I knew of it through my Voices. I had never seen the men who went to look for it. I wrote to the churchmen of Fierbois, and asked them to let me have it, and they sent it. It was not deep in the earth; it was behind the altar, as I think, but I am not certain whether it was in front of the altar or behind it. I think I wrote that it was behind it. When it was found, the clergy rubbed it, and the rust readily fell off. The man who brought it was a merchant of

Tours who sold armour. The clergy of Fierbois gave me a sheath; the people of Tours gave me two, one of red velvet, one of cloth of gold, but I had a strong leather sheath made for it." [1]

A household (*état*) was provided for Joan by the Dauphin's command. She was to have a confessor, an equerry, two pages: the faithful Jean de Metz was her treasurer. Poulangy, the second (chronologically) of her knights, was also of the company. She asked for a standard: St. Margaret and St. Catherine, she told the Dauphin, had commanded her to take a standard and bear it valiantly. The King of Heaven was to be painted on it, said the crowned and gracious ladies. Furthermore, "the world was painted on it" (which Andrew Lang takes to have been "the globe in the hand of our Lord"), an angel on either side. The stuff was white linen dotted with lilies: the motto *Jesus Maria*. In action, the Maid always carried this standard, that she might "strike no man with the sword; she never slew any man. The personal blazon of the Maid was a shield azure with a white dove, bear-

[1] Lang. "Maid of France, p. 99.

ing in its beak a scroll whereon was written, *De par le Roy du ciel."* [1]

So, at long last, the word was "Forward!"

On March 6th, as we have seen, Joan of Arc left Vaucouleurs, a humble figure in black and gray, between two faithful but obscure men-at-arms; now, nine weeks later, she rides out in radiant armor, silver-white from head to foot, in her hand the snowy standard with its sacred emblems, on either side nobles and dignitaries of the Court of France So she rides, and the hearts of men follow her

[1] Lang "Maid of France," p 99

CHAPTER IX

ORLEANS

WE do not know the precise numbers of the army that Joan brought to the relief of Orleans; it was probably under four thousand men. Of the army already there, Dunois said that two hundred Englishmen could put to flight eight hundred or a thousand French The latter were utterly discouraged and hardly attempted resistance. On the other hand the English, sure of their victory, had grown careless and lazy. True, they had pricked up their ears when word came of the Maid and her mission; but weeks passed, and nothing happened. When they chased the French the latter ran away as usual: they were somewhat bored, and thought it about time to finish, and wind up the siege. Inside the walls, people awaited the Maid as those who look for the morning.

She left Tours, as we have seen, and came to Blois, where she was joined by La Hire,

Gilles de Rais, and others. There was some delay here, owing to lack of money for the expenses of the journey. Charles had before this been obliged to pawn the *"fleurons"* of his crown and the gold ornaments of his helmet to obtain ready money. By these means or others he now raised the needed sum, and the army, with its "great convoy of cattle and grain"[1] moved on once more. A company of priests had joined them, and Joan insisted that every man-at-arms must make confession before going into action. When they left Blois the clergy went first, singing "Come, holy Spirit!" So, on April 28th, the Maid and her army found themselves opposite Orleans. on the other side of the river. Dunois, who had been watching from the battlements, took boat and went across to greet the Maid; he found her in angry mood. She had expected to find herself at the city gates, not with a broad and swift stream flowing between Moreover, she had been suffering much pain from the weight of her armor, which she had worn all day. She greeted the leader abruptly.

"Are you the Bastard of Orleans?"

[1] Lang

"I am, and right glad of your coming."

"Was it you who gave counsel to come by this bank of the river, so that I cannot go straight against Talbot and the English?"

"I, and others wiser than I, gave that counsel, and I think it the wiser way and the safer."

"In God's name, the counsel of our Lord is wiser and safer than yours. You think to deceive me, and you deceive yourself, for I bring you better rescue than ever came to knight or city; the succor of the King of Heaven."

Dunois himself says that as she spoke the words, "in a moment the wind, which was contrary and strong, shifted and became favorable." This, to the soldier's mind, was a manifest miracle. He begged Joan to cross with him. She demurred, not wishing to leave her army, which must return to Blois for another convoy. Without her they might go astray, might fall into sin, possibly might not return. Dunois persisted, implored; the city was awaiting her; the need was desperate. Let the captains go without her! Joan yielded to his entreaties; the captains departed, prom-

ising to return in good time; the Maid crossed
the river with a force of two hundred lances,
the wind so favoring them that every third
vessel towed two others. Seeing this, all the
bystanders were of Dunois' mind; "A miracle
of God!"

So, about eight o'clock on the evening of
April 29th, Joan of Arc entered Orleans.

The *"Journal du Siège d'Orléans,"* kept by
a citizen whose name is lost, thus describes
the entry. The Maid rode "in full armor,
mounted on a white horse, with her pennon
carried before her, which was white, also, and
bore two angels, each holding a lily in his
hand; on the pennon was painted an Annunciation. At her left side rode the Bastard of
Orleans in armor, richly appointed, and behind
her came many other noble and valiant lords
and squires, captains and soldiers, with the
burghers of Orleans who had gone out to
escort her. At the gate there came to meet
her the rest of the soldiers, with the men and
women of Orleans, carrying many torches, and
rejoicing as if they had seen God descend
among them; not without cause. For they had
endured much weariness and labor and pain,

and, what is worse, great fear lest they should never be succored, but should lose both life and goods. Now all felt greatly comforted and, as it were, already unbesieged, through the divine virtue of which they had heard in this simple maid; whom they regarded right lovingly, both men and women, and likewise the little children. There was a marvelous press to touch her, and to touch even the horse on which she rode, while a torch-bearer came so near her pennon that it was set afire. Thereupon she struck her horse with her spurs and put out the fire, turning the horse gently toward the pennon, just as if she had been long a warrior, which the soldiers thought a very wonderful thing, and the burghers also. These accompanied her the whole length of the city with right good cheer, and with great honor they all escorted her to the house of James Boucher, treasurer of the Duke of Orleans, where she was received with great joy." [1]

In this honored and patriarchal household, Joan, "venerated like an angel sent from heaven," passed the week of the Deliverance. It was to this friendly hearth that she went

[1] Trans F C Lowell.

whenever a breathing-space allowed her to return within the walls.

At these times, the press of people about the house would almost break the doors in. The kindly household protected, cherished, revered their gentle guest. When Jacques Boucher died, some thirteen years later, the monument raised to his memory by his widow and children recorded, with his name and rank, the fact that he had received into his house, as a revered guest, "the Maid, by God's help the saviour of the city."

On the evening of her arrival she supped on a few slices of bread dipped in wine and water. She begged that her host's daughter Charlotte, a child of ten years, might share her couch. Every morning, crossing the garden to the neighboring church, she assisted at mass, prayed for the relief of the city, and received with tears the holy communion.

On Tuesday, May 3rd, a solemn procession, led by the Maid, went to the cathedral to pray for the deliverance of the city. Here she was met by a priest, "Dr. John of Mascon, a very wise man," who looked at her in pity and in wonder.

"My child," he asked, "are you come hither to raise the siege?"

"In God's name, yes, my father!"

The good father shook his head sadly.

"My child, they are strong, and strongly fenced; it would be a mighty feat of arms to dislodge them."

"To the power of God," replied Joan, "nothing is impossible!"

This was her word, on this and on all days.

"Throughout the city," says the old chronicle, "she rendered honour to no one else!" The learned Doctor bowed his head, and from that moment accepted her as a messenger of God.

The Maid's arrival was followed by a brief lull in hostilities. She would not raise her sword till she had duly summoned the enemy, and bidden him depart in peace. On April 2nd she despatched the letter already quoted. The English replied promptly that if they caught the so-called Maid, they would burn her for a witch. In the evening of the same day, she went out on the bridge, and mounting on the barricades, called to Glasdale and his garrison, bidding them obey God and surrender, and promising to spare their lives if they would do so. They replied with a torrent of abuse and ridicule. "Milkmaid" was the gentlest term they had for her. They showed a bold front, Glasdale, Talbot, de la Pole and the rest; but they were ill at ease. They knew that their men were full of superstitious forebodings. They themselves were strangely shaken at sight of the slender girlish figure in snow-white armor, at sound of the clear ringing voice calling on them to fear God and yield to his Emissary. They could and did answer defiantly, but they attempted nothing more. On Monday, May 2d, Joan summoned them again, and again their only answer was gibes and insults. She rode out, a great multitude following her, to reconnoitre the enemy's position; rode about and about the various bastilles, noting every angle, every turret, every embrasure for cannon. The English watched her, but never stirred. Talbot, the old lion, victor in a score of fights, must have ground his teeth at the sight; but either he dared not trust his men, or else knew them to be outnumbered. He lay still, while the gallant little cavalcade, priests chanting in front, white-robed Maid in the midst, lifting her snowy standard, delirious people thronging to touch her stirrup, swept past their camp, and re-entered the city. A bitter hour for John Talbot!

Joan was delaying her attack till the army should return from Blois with the second convoy. On May 3d they appeared; at dawn on the fourth, Joan rode out with five hundred men to meet them; by noon all were safe within the walls, and the Maid sat down quietly to dinner with her faithful squire d'Aulon. They were still sitting when Dunois came in with news that Sir John Fastolf, the hero of the Battle of the Herrings, was but a day's march distant with provisions and reinforcements for the English.

Joan received the tidings joyfully. "In God's name, Bastard," she said, "I charge you to let me know as soon as you hear of his arrival. Should he pass without my knowledge —I will have your head!"

"Have no fear of that!" said Dunois. "You shall have the news the instant it comes."

Weary with her ride, and her heavy armor, the Maid lay down beside her hostess to rest.

D'Aulon curled up on a little couch in the corner of the room; both slept as tired people do

Suddenly the Maid sprang up, calling loudly to d'Aulon.

"In God's name," she cried, "I must go against the English. My Voices call me, I know not whether it is against their forts, or Fastolf comes."

Bewildered and full of sleep, d'Aulon and good Mme. Boucher helped her into her armor; even as they did so, voices rose in the street, crying that the English were attacking with great slaughter. She ran downstairs and met her page, Louis de Coulet.

"Miserable boy," she cried; "the blood of France is shedding, and you do not call me? My horse on the instant!"

The boy flew for the horse; the Maid mounted, calling for her banner, which he handed to her from an upper window, and rode off at full speed, squire and page following as best they might.

It was not Fastolf. Unknown to the Maid, certain of the French had planned an attack on the fort of St. Loup, about a mile and a half from the town. Either ignorant or careless of

Dunois' promise to the Maid, they rode merrily to the attack, and surrounded the fort with
warlike shouts. Out swarmed the English like
angry bees; swords flashed; the struggle was
sharp but brief. The French, with no adequate
leader, gave back before the rush of the defenders; broke, turned, and were streaming
pell-mell back toward the city, when they saw
the Maid galloping toward them. Alone she
rode; her snowy armor gleaming, her snowy
standard fluttering. In the gateway she paused
a moment at sight of a wounded man borne
past by his comrades. She never could look
on French blood without a pang: "My hair
rises for horror," she would say. But only a
moment; the next, she had met the retreating
troops; rallied them, led them once more to
the assault. They followed her shouting, every
man eager to ride beside her, or at least within
sight of her, within sound of her silver voice.
On to the fort once more! this time with God
and the messenger of God!

The English saw and in their turn faltered;
wavered; gave back before the furious onset;
broke and fled in disorder. The French pursued them to the fort, which they captured and

burned. The church of St. Loup hard by had already been partly destroyed, but Joan forbade the plundering of it, and spared the lives of certain English soldiers who had thought to escape by arraying themselves in priestly vestments which they had found in the church. "We must not rob the clergy," she said merrily.

The French losses in this affair were insignificant; the English force, about one hundred and fifty men, were all either killed or captured. The victorious Maid rode back to the city, to weep for those who had died unshriven, and to confess her sins to Father Pasquerel, her director.

She told her followers that the siege would be raised in five days. The next day, Thursday May 5th, was Ascension Day, and she would not fight. Instead, she summoned the enemy once more. Crossing to the end of the bridge, where a small fort had been erected, she called across the water to the English in the Tourelles, bidding them depart in peace It was God's will, she said simply, that they should go. They replied with the usual gibes and insults On this, she dictated a formal summons, ending with these words: "This is the third and last time that I write to you. I would have sent my letter in more honorable fashion, but you keep my herald, Guienne. Return him, and I will return the prisoners taken at St. Loup."

The letter was bound round the shaft of an arrow, and shot from the bridge into the English camp. An Englishman picked it up, crying, "News from the harlot of the Armagnacs!"

Joan wept at these brutal words, and called on the King of Heaven to comfort her; almost immediately thereupon she was of good cheer, "because she had tidings from her Lord"; and without wasting time began to make ready for the morrow.

Early Friday morning (May 6th) troops and citizens issued through the Burgundy gate, crossed the river in boats, and advanced upon the Tourelles. This little fort had been restored by the English, and was now a strong place, with its pierced walls and its boulevard, and the fortified convent of the Augustines hard by. As the French advanced, the English sallied forth to meet them, in such numbers and with so bold a front that the assailants wavered, and began to fall back toward the island on which the central part of the bridge rested. This troop was commanded by De Gaucourt, the governor of the city, an old man and timid. Seeing his men and himself in danger, he would have withdrawn with them, but at the moment a cry was heard: "The Maid! the Maid!" Joan and La Hire had brought their horses over by boat, and now were galloping to the rescue, after them soldiers and townspeople in a rush. De Gaucourt would have held his soldiers back, but in vain.

"You are an evil man!" cried the Maid. "Will you nill you, the men-at-arms will follow me to victory!"

On she swept, lance in rest, crying, "In God's name, forward! forward boldly!" On swept La Hire and the rest, De Gaucourt and his men with them, carried away body and soul of them by the impetuous rush. They charged the English and drove them back to their intrenchments. Many of the defenders were slain, many taken; the rest took refuge in the boulevard, or outwork of the Tourelles.

Many of the victorious French remained on the spot, to guard against a possible night assault. Mounting guard in the captured

Augustine convent, they supped on provisions brought to them in boats from the city, and slept on their arms, tired but joyful men.

The Maid, however, had been wounded in the foot by a calthrop, and was besides mortally weary She went back to Orleans, to the kindly shelter of the Boucher roof. It was Friday; she usually fasted on that day, but this time she felt the absolute need of food. To-morrow was before her, when she must have her full strength; she must eat, must rest; for this reason she had come back, though her heart was full of anxiety, dreading the night attack which her keen military sense told her the enemy might and ought to make. But the enemy was tired, too, and discouraged to boot: no attack came.

"Rouse ye at daybreak to-morrow!" she charged her followers. "You shall do better still than to-day. Keep by my side, for I have much to do more than ever I had, and blood will flow from my body, above my breast."

Then the good Maid said her prayers, and lay down quietly to rest, and to such sleep as her wound and her anxious heart would allow.

CHAPTER X

THE RELIEF

ANXIOUS indeed was this night for the
Maid. Her unerring instinct told her
that the English should make a counter attack,
under cover of night, on the weary French,
sleeping on their arms under the open sky or
in the ruined Augustines, the broad stream
flowing between them and safety. This, all
authorities agree, they ought to have done;
exactly why they did not do it, perhaps John
Talbot alone knows. We know only that the
night passed quietly, and that at sunrise on
May seventh Joan heard mass and set forth
on her high errand.

"There is much to do!" she said. "More
than I ever had yet!"

Much indeed! The "boulevard" had high
walls, and could be approached only by scaling-
ladders; round it was a deep ditch or fosse.
Beyond stood the Tourelles, still more strongly

fortified. To take these two strongholds in the face of Talbot and his bulldogs was a heavy task indeed; but Joan was full of confidence and cheer. As she mounted her horse, a man brought her *"une alose"* a sea-trout or shad, for her breakfast.

"Keep it for supper!" said the Maid merrily to good Père Boucher, her friendly host. "I will bring back a 'goddam' to eat it with me; and I shall bring him back across the bridge!"

So she rode out, with her captains about her on either side, Dunois, and La Hire, De Gaucourt, Xaintrailles and the rest, a valiant company. One chronicler says that the captains went unwillingly, thinking the odds heavy against them. One would rather think that they shared their girl-leader's confidence; surely Dunois and La Hire did. They crossed the river in boats, and with them every man who could be spared from the city, which must be guarded from a possible attack by Talbot. French men-at-arms, Scottish and Italian mercenaries, citizens and apprentices, flocked to the banner of the Maid, armed with guns, crossbows, clubs, or whatever weapon came to hand; carrying great shields, too, and movable sheds to shelter their advance.

Inside the forts, six hundred English yeomen awaited them with confidence equal to their own. They were well armed; their great gun *Passe Volant* could throw an eighty-pound stone ball across the river and into the city; moreover, they had possession, that necessary nine points of the law, and English hearts for the tenth part; small wonder they were confident.

It was still early morning when the French rushed to the assault, planting their scaling ladders along the walls, wherever foothold could be found; swarming up them like bees, shouting, cutting, slashing, receiving cut and slash in return.

"Well the English fought," says the old chronicle, "for the French were scaling at once in various places, in thick swarms, attacking on the highest parts of their walls, with such hardihood and valor, that to see them you would have thought they deemed themselves immortal. But the English drove them back many times, and tumbled them from high to low; fighting with bowshot and gunshot, with axes, lances, bills, and leaden maces, and even with their fists, so that there was some loss in killed and wounded."[1]

Smoke and flame, shouts and cries, hissing of bolts and whistling bullets, with now and then the crash of the great stone balls; a wild scene; and always in the front rank the Maid, her white banner floating under the wall, her clear voice calling, directing, thrilling all who heard it.

So through the morning the fight raged. About noon a bolt or arrow struck her, the point passing through steel and flesh, and standing out a handbreadth behind her shoulder.

"She shrank and wept," says Father Pasquerel; but she would not have a charm sung over the wound to stay the bleeding. "I would rather die," she said, "than so sin against the will of God."[2]

She prayed, and feeling her strength returning, drew out the arrow with her own hand.

Dunois thinks she paid no further attention to the wound, and went on fighting till evening; but Father Pasquerel says she had it dressed with olive oil, and paused long enough to confess to him.

The English, seeing the Maid wounded, took heart even as the French lost it. The day was passing; "the place, to all men of the sword, seemed impregnable." [1]

"Doubt not!" cried the Maid, "the place is ours!"

But even Dunois held that "there was no hope of victory this day." He gave orders to sound the recall and withdraw the troops across the river. The day was lost?

Not so! "But then," he says, "the Maid came to me, and asked me to wait yet a little while. Then she mounted her horse, and went alone into the vineyard, some way from the throng of men, and in that vineyard she abode in prayer for about a quarter of an hour. Then she came back, and straightway took her standard into her hands and planted it on the edge of the fosse."

Seeing her once more in her place, steel and iron having apparently no power upon her, the English "shuddered, and fear fell upon them." They too, remember, had had their prophecies.

[1] Percival de Cagny.

"A virgin would mount on the backs of their archers!" A month, a week ago, they had still laughed at this. Now the "mysterious consolation" which seemed to radiate from the person of the Maid on all faithful Frenchmen, heartening and uplifting them, became for her adversaries a mysterious terror, striking cold on the stoutest heart.

The French had already sounded the retreat; the banner of the Maid, borne all day long by her faithful standard-bearer d'Aulon, had already been handed by him to a comrade for the withdrawal; when at Joan's earnest prayer the recall was countermanded.

D'Aulon said to his friend, a Basque whom he knew well, "If I dismount and go forward to the foot of the wall, will you follow me?"

He sprang from his saddle, held up his shield against the shower of arrows, and leaped into the ditch, supposing that the Basque was following him. The Maid at this moment saw her standard in the hands of the Basque, who also had gone down into the ditch. She seems not to have recognized his purpose. She thought that her standard was

lost, or was being betrayed, and seized the end
of the floating flag.

"Ha! my standard! my standard!" she cried,
and she so shook the flag that it waved wildly
like a signal for instant onset. The men-at-
arms conceived it to be such a signal, and
gathered for attack.

"Ha! Basque, is this what you promised
me?" cried d'Aulon. Thereon the Basque tore
the flag from the hands of the Maid, ran
through the ditch, and stood beside d'Aulon,
close to the enemy's wall. By this time the
whole company of those who loved her had
rallied and were round her.

"Watch!" said Joan to a knight at her
side, "Watch till the tail of my standard
touches the wall!"

A few moments passed.

"Joan, the flag touches the wall!"

"Then enter, all is yours!" [1]

Then, like a wave of the sea, the French
flung themselves upon the ladders; scaled the
wall, mounted the crest, leaped or fell down
on the inside; cut, thrust, hacked, all with such
irresistible fury that the English, after valiant

[1] A. Lang, p 122

resistance, finally turned and fled to the draw-bridge that crossed to the Tourelles.

Ah! The bridge was in flames! Smoke rolled over it, tongues of flame shot out red between the planks.

Seeing this, Joan's heart went out to the men who had wronged and insulted her, yet had fought so valiantly.

"Glasdale!" she cried; "Glasdale! yield thee to the King of Heaven! Thou calledst me harlot, but I have great pity on thy soul and the souls of thy company!"

Glasdale, brave as he was brutal, made no answer, but turned to meet a new peril, dire indeed. The people of the city had made a fireship and loaded it with inflammable material, lighted the mass, and towed it all flaming under the wooden drawbridge. The bridge flared to heaven, yet with heroic courage Glasdale and a handful of his knights shepherded the greater part of the defenders of the lost boulevard over the burning bridge, back into the stone enclosure of the Tourelles, themselves meantime holding the bridge with axe and sword.

The fugitives reached the fort only to find

themselves assailed from a new quarter. Those watching the fight saw with amazement and terror men crossing from the city to the Tourelles, apparently through the air, over a gap where two arches were broken. A miracle? No, only quickness of wit and action. An old gutter had been found and laid across the gap, and over this frail support walked the Prior of the Knights of Malta, followed by his men-at-arms.

Finding all lost but honor, Glasdale and his faithful few turned and leaped on the burning drawbridge, hoping to make good their retreat into the fort The charred beams broke under them, and borne down by their heavy armor, the brave English sank beneath the tide, while on the bank the "Witch of the Armagnacs" knelt weeping, and prayed for their souls.

Dunois, La Hire, and the rest were more concerned at losing so much good ransom.

For all was over; of all the valiant defenders of the two forts, not one man escaped death or captivity.

The red flames lit up the ruined forts; in Orleans the joy bells rang their wildest peal;

and over the bridge, as she had promised, "crossing on ill-laid planks and half-broken arches," the Maid of Orleans rode back to the city she had saved.

Seventeen years old; a peasant maiden, who could not read or write, she had fought and won one of the "fifteen decisive battles of the world."

CHAPTER XI

THE DELIVERANCE

IT was eight o'clock on the evening of the
eighth of May when the people of Orleans
gathered in dense masses at the bridgehead and
along the riverside to greet their rescuer.
Dusk had fallen; they pressed forward with
lanterns and torches held aloft, all striving for
a sight of the Maid.

"By these flickering lights," says Jules
Quicherat, "Joan seemed to them beautiful as
the angel conqueror of a demon."

Yet it was not the morning vision of snow
and silver, fresh and dewy as her own youth,
that had ridden out at daybreak to battle.
Weary now was the white charger, drooping
his gallant neck; weary was the Maid, faint
with the pain of her wound, her white armor
dinted and stained. But the people of Orleans
saw nothing save their Angel of Deliverance.
They pressed round her, eager to touch her
armor, her floating standard, the horse which

had borne her so bravely through the day. Weary and wounded as she was, she smiled on one and all, and "in the sweetest feminine voice, called them good Christians, and assured them that God would save them."

So she rode on to the Cathedral, where she returned thanks humbly and devoutly to God who had given the victory; then, still surrounded by the shouting, rejoicing throng, home to the house of Boucher, where they left her

"There was not a man who, going home after this evening, did not feel in him the strength of ten Englishmen."[1]

She had fasted since dawn, but she was too tired to eat the *alose*, nor did she bring the promised "goddam" to share it with her. The goddams were all dead save a few, who were jealously guarded for ransom. She supped on a few bits of bread dipped in weak wine and water, and a surgeon came and dressed her wound.

All night, we are told, the joy bells rang through the rescued city, while the good Maid slept with the peace of Heaven in her heart.

[1] Quicherat

It was not a long sleep. At daybreak came tidings that the English had issued from their tents and arrayed themselves in order of battle.

Instantly Joan arose and dressed, putting on a light coat of chain mail, as her wounded shoulder could not bear the weight of the heavy plate armor. She rode out with Dunois and the rest, and the French order of battle was formed, fronting the English; so the two armies remained for the space of an hour. The French, full of the strong wine of yesterday's victory, were eager to attack; but Joan held them back. "If they attack us," she said, "fight bravely and we shall conquer them; but do not begin the battle!"

Then she did a strange thing. She sent for a priest, and bade him celebrate mass in front of the army; and that done, to celebrate it yet again. Both services "she and all the soldiers heard with great devotion."

"Now," said the Maid, "look well, and tell me; are their faces set toward us?"

"No!" was the reply. "They have turned their backs on us, and their faces are set toward Meung."

"In God's name, they are gone!" said Joan.

"Let them go, and let us go and praise God, and follow them no farther, since this is Sunday."

"Whereupon," says the chronicle, "the Maid with the other lords and soldiers returned to Orleans with great joy, to the great triumph of all the clergy and people, who with one accord returned to our Lord humble thanks and praises well deserved for the victory he had given them over the English, the ancient enemies of this realm." [1]

This service of thanksgiving ordered by Joan of Arc on the ninth of May, 1429, was the virtual foundation of the great festival which Orleans has now celebrated with hardly a break for five hundred years.

After that first outbreak of thanksgiving, Dunois himself laid down the rules for the annual keeping of the festival, which are given in the "Chronicle of the establishment of the *fête*," written thirty years after the siege.

"My lord the bishop of Orleans, and my lord Dunois (the Bastard), brother of my lord the duke of Orleans, with the duke's advice, as well as the burghers and inhabitants of the

[1] Translated by F C Lowell

145

said Orleans, ordered that on the eighth of
May there should be a procession of people
carrying candles, which procession should
march as far as the Augustines, and, wherever
the fight had raged, there a halt should be
made and a suitable service should be had in
each place with prayer. We cannot give too
much praise to God and the Saints, since all
that was done by God's grace, and so, with
great devotion, we ought to take part in the
said procession. Even the men of Bourges
and of certain other cities celebrate the day,
because if Orleans had fallen into the hands
of the English, the rest of the kingdom would
have taken great harm. Always remembering,
therefore, the great mercy which God has
shown to the said city of Orleans, we ought
always to maintain and never to abandon this
holy procession, lest we fall into ingratitude,
whereby much evil may come upon us. Every
one is obliged to join the said procession, carrying a lighted candle in his hand. It passes
round about the town in front of the church
of our Lady of Saint Paul, at which place they
sing praises to our Lady; and it goes thence
to the cathedral, where the sermon is preached,

and thereafter a mass is sung. There are also vigils at Saint Aignan, and, on the morrow, a mass for the dead. All men, therefore, should be bidden to praise God and to thank Him; for at the present time there are youths who can hardly believe that the thing came about in this wise; you, however, should believe that this is a true thing, and is verily the great grace of God." [1]

Walls and boulevard have long since been outgrown by the city of the Loire: dynasties have risen and fallen, wars have swept and harried France after their fashion. Still, in the early May time, when Nature is fair and young and sweet as the Maid herself, Orleans rises up to do reverence to her rescuer. The priests walk in holiday vestments, the bells ring out, the censers swing, the people throng the streets and fill the churches.

During her brief stay in Orleans after its deliverance, Joan bore herself with her own quiet modesty. She loved solitude, and rather shunned than sought company. She took no credit to herself; the glory was God's and

[1] Translated by F C Lowell

God's alone, she repeatedly told the people, who flocked about her in adoration.

"Never were seen such deeds as you have wrought!" they told her. "No book tells of such marvels!"

"My Lord," replied the Maid, "has a book in which no clerk ever read, were he ever so clerkly."[1]

What next was for the Maid to do?

Orleans was delivered, but France was still under English rule. John of Bedford, "brave soldier, prudent captain, skilful diplomatist, having experience of camps and courts," was startled, but not discouraged by the rescue of Orleans. He meant to rule France for his child-king, and to rule it well; as a matter of fact, he did rule it for thirteen years, striving always "in a degree superior to his century," to bring order out of chaos, to convert the bloodstained wilderness of the conquered country into a decent and well-ordered realm.

Nor was John Talbot himself one whit disheartened. He had lost some of his best men on the bloody day of the Tourelles, but he had

[1] Pasquerel, translated by F C. Lowell.

plenty more. He had lost Orleans, but the river towns on either side of it were still his, Meung, Beaugency, Jargeau; all strongly fortified, all guarding river and high road so that no man might pass without their leave.

He had retreated in excellent order from that field where his offered battle had been—strangely, he may have thought—refused by the Maid and her victorious army; he now established himself at Meung, with strong outposts at Beaugency and Jargeau, and awaited the next move on the enemy's part.

Bedford, meantime, assembled in all haste another army at Paris, prepared to go to Talbot's assistance whenever need should arise.

Joan knew better than to follow the orderly retreat of the English. Her own men, with all their superb courage, even with the flame of victory in their hearts, had not the training necessary for a long campaign in the open; neither was there money for it, nor provisions.

Besides, her Voices had but one message for her now; she was to go to the Dauphin; he was to be crowned king, as soon as might be; then—to Paris!

Leaving Dunois in charge of Orleans, Joan,

with several of her followers, rode out once more, this time to Tours, whither Charles came from Chinon to meet her.

It was a strange meeting. The conquering Maid, she beside whom, as she and all her followers believed, the angels of God had fought for France, rode forward, bareheaded, her glorious banner drooping in her hand, and bent humbly to her saddle-bow in obeisance. Charles bade her sit erect;[1] an eyewitness thinks that in his joy he fain would have kissed her. He might better have alighted and held her stirrup, but this would naturally not occur to him; certainly not to the Maid, who had but one thought in her loyal heart.

"Gentle Dauphin," she said, "let us make haste and be gone to Rheims, where you shall be crowned king!" Now, she pleaded, was the time, while their enemies still "fled, so to speak, from themselves."[1]

She added some words which well had it been for Charles if he had heeded. "I shall hardly last more than a year!" she said. "We must think about working right well this year, for there is much to do."

From the beginning, she had known that her time was short. The how and why were mercifully hidden from her, but she knew right well that whatever she was to do must be done soon.

But Charles of Valois would not willingly do anything one year that might be put off till the next. He hesitated; dawdled; consulted La Trémoille, his favorite and master: consulted Jean Gerson, the *most Christian doctor,* whom men called the wisest Frenchman of his age. The latter gave full honor and credence to the Maid. "Even if (which God forbid) she should be mistaken," he wrote, "in her hopes and ours, it would not necessarily follow that what she does comes of the evil spirit and not of God, but that rather our ingratitude was to blame. Let the party which hath a just cause take care how by incredulity or injustice it rendereth useless the divine succor so miraculously manifested, for God, without any change of counsel, changeth the upshot according to desert." [1]

Thus Gerson, the learned and saintly. La Trémoille, the ignorant and unscrupulous, was

[1] Guizot

of another mind, and La Trémoille was master
of the Dauphin and of such part of France as
the Dauphin ruled. This greedy parasite had
been willing that Orleans should be rescued;
that alone boded him no special danger. Any
general awakening of the country, however,
any dawn of hope, freedom, tranquillity, for
the unhappy people, might be disastrous for
him. While the strength of the realm was
expended on petty squabbles among Charles's
various adherents, while the splitting of hairs
with Burgundy filled the time safely and agree-
ably, La Trémoille could rob and squeeze the
people at his pleasure. But now affairs began
to take on a new aspect. This Maid, having
saved Orleans, might well have busied herself
with matters of personal glory and profit. Instead of this, she talked of nothing but a
united France, a France at peace, with honor;
of Charles a king indeed, with all good and
true men serving him honestly and joyfully.
Moreover, his, La Trémoille's, chief rival and
former patron, Arthur of Brittany, Count of
Richemont, was an admirer of this troublesome
young woman.

Altogether it seemed to La Trémoille that

the Maid was not a person to be encouraged. Fair and softly, though; no haste, no outward show of enmity, judicious procrastination could do much.

Procrastination suited Charles admirably; he asked nothing better. He dawdled two precious weeks away at Tours; then he went to Loches, and dawdled there. (His son, Louis XI. did *not* dawdle at Loches, though he spent much time there, making cages for unruly cardinals, worshipping our Lady of Embrun, hanging men like apples on his orchard trees, and otherwise disporting himself in his own fashion! But that was thirty years later.)

Poor Joan, bewildered at this strange way of following up a great victory, followed Charles to Loches, and with Dunois at her side sought the Dauphin in his apartments, where he was talking with his confessor and two other members of his council, Robert le Maçon and Christopher of Harcourt.

Entering the room, with a modest but determined mien she knelt before Charles and clasped his knees.

"Noble Dauphin," she said, "do not hold so many and such lengthy councils, but come at once to Rheims and take the crown that is yours!"

Upon this, Harcourt asked her if this advice came from her *"conseil,"* as she called her heavenly advisers. "Yes!" she replied. "They greatly insist thereupon."

"Will you not tell us, in the presence of the king, what is the nature and manner of this counsel that you receive?"

Joan blushed; it was great pain to her to unveil things so sacred; but she answered bravely: "I understand well enough what it is you wish to know, and I will tell you freely.

"When men do not believe in those things which come to me from God, it grieves me sore. Then I go apart and pray, making my plaint to my Lord for that they are so hard of belief: and after I have prayed I hear a Voice saying to me, 'Child of God, go, go, go! I will be thy helper; go!'[1] When I hear that Voice I am joyful, and wish it might always be thus with me."

While she spoke, she raised her eyes to heaven, and seemed indeed in an ecstasy of joy.

[1] *Fille Dé, va, va, va! je serai à ton aide, va!*

Charles listened, was impressed, and doubtless went to tell La Trémoille about it.

But there were others, who cared nothing for La Trémoille and much for the Maid. The young Duke of Alençon was, we know, her sworn brother-in-arms. He had no mind to let the glory of Orleans evaporate in trailing mists of negotiation and dispute. He got together a little army, and demanded the presence and help of the Maid in a campaign against the English. La Trémoille could not well prevent this; he could only so manage that a whole month was wasted before permission was given. This was a hard month for the Maid To her eyes it was clear as the sun in heaven that "when once the Dauphin was crowned and consecrated, the power of his adversaries would continually dwindle."

"All," says Dunois, "came to share her opinion!" By which he meant all true and knightly persons like himself.

Finally the matter was decided. A rendezvous was appointed at Selles, not far from Loches; thither, in the first days of June, the Maid repaired, and there gathered about her all the chivalry of France, eager to follow her to fresh conquests.

Alençon was in command; he was, we might say, the temporal chief; Joan the spiritual one. Dunois was there; La Hire, Vendôme, and the rest; among them Guy de Laval and his brother Andrew. A letter from the former, written in his name and his brother's to his mother and grandmother, has been preserved, and gives us so clear and life-like a picture of the occasion and of Joan herself that I cannot resist giving it in full. *Mutatis mutandis,* it is not so unlike certain letters that come over the sea to-day.[1] Reading it, we can thrill with the two women, one of whom, remember, the grandmother, was the widow of Bertrand Du Guesclin.

My Reverend Ladies and Mothers· After I wrote you on Friday last from St. Catherine of Fierbois, I reached Loches on Saturday, and went to see my lord Dauphin[2] in the castle, after vespers in the collegiate church. He is a very fair and gracious lord, very well made and active, and ought to be about seven years old. Sunday I came to St Aignan, where the king was, and I sen⁺ for my lord of Treves to come to my quarters; and my uncle went up with him to the castle to tell the king I was come, and to find out when he would be pleased to have me wait on him. I got the answer that I should go as soon as I wished, and he greeted me kindly and said many pleasant things to me On Monday I left the king to go to Selles, four leagues from St Aignan, and the king sent for the Maid, who was then at Selles Some people said that this was done for my sake, so that I could see her; at any rate she was very pleasant to my brother and me, being fully armed, except for her head, and holding her lance in her hand Afterwards, when we had dismounted at Selles, I went to her quarters to see her, and she had wine brought, and told me she would soon serve it to me in Paris, and what she did seemed at times quite divine, both to look at her and to hear her Monday at vespers she left Selles to go to Romorantin, three leagues in advance, the marshal of Boussac and a great many soldiers and common people being with her I saw her get on horseback, armed all in white, except her head, with a little battle-axe in her hand, riding a great black courser, which was very restive at the door of her lodgings, and would not let her mount. So she said, "Lead him to the cross," which was in front of the church near by, in the road. There she mounted without his budging, just as if he had been tied, and then she turned toward the church door which was close by, and said, "You priests and churchmen, make a procession and pray to God " She then set out on the road, calling "Forward, forward," with her little battle-axe in her hand, and her waving banner carried by a pretty page

On Monday my lord duke of Alençon came to Selles with a great company, and to-day I won a match from him at tennis I found here a gentleman sent from my brother Chauvigny, because he had heard that I had reached St. Catherine. The man said that he had summoned his vassals and expected soon to be here, and that he still loved my sister dearly, and that she was stouter than she used to be It is said here that my lord constable is coming with six hundred men at arms and four hundred archers, and that the king never had so great a force as they hope to gather. But there is no money at court, or so little that for the present I can expect no help nor maintenance; so since you have my seal, my lady mother, do not hesitate to sell or mortgage my lands, or else make some other provision by which we may be saved; otherwise through our own fault we shall be dishonored, and perhaps come near perishing, since if we do not do something of the kind, as there is no pay, we shall be left quite alone So far we have been, and we are still, much honored, and our coming has greatly pleased the king and all his people, and they make us better cheer than you could imagine.

The Maid told me in her lodgings, when I went there to see her, that three days before my coming she had sent to you, my grandmother, a little gold ring, but she said that it was a very little thing and that she would willingly have sent you something better considering your rank.

To-day my lord of Alençon, the Bastard of Orleans, and Gaucourt should leave this place of Selles, and go after the Maid, and you have sent I don't know what letters to my cousin La Trémoille and to my lord of Treves, so that the king wants to keep me with him until the Maid has been before the English places around Orleans to which they are going to lay siege, and the artillery is already prepared, and the Maid makes no doubt that she will soon be with the king, saying that when he starts to advance towards Rheims I shall go with him; but God forbid that I should do this, and not go with her at once, and my brother says so, too, and so does my lord of Alençon—

such a good-for-nothing will a fellow be who stay behind. They think that the king will leave here to-day, to draw nearer to the army, and men are coming in from all directions every day. They hope that before ten days are out affairs will be nearly settled one way or the other, but all have so good hope in God that I believe He will help us.

My very respected ladies and mothers, we send our remembrances, my brother and I, to you, as humbly as we can; and please also write us at once news of yourselves, and do you, my lady mother, tell me how you find yourself after the medicines you have taken, for I am much troubled about you

My very respected ladies and mothers, I pray the blessed son of God to give you a good life and a long one, and we both of us also send our remembrances to our brother Louis. Written at Selles this Wednesday the 8th of June.

And this vespers there came here my lord of Vendôme, my lord of Boussac, and others, and La Hire is close to the army, and soon they will get to work. God grant that we get our wish.

Your humble sons,
Guy and Andrew of Laval [1]

On June 9th, Alençon and the Maid entered Orleans with their army, about two thousand strong. The people flocked about her with joyous greetings and offers of provisions and munitions; they could not do enough to show their enduring gratitude to the saviour of

[1] Lowell, pp 120-123.

159

their beloved city. Beside this, it must be confessed that they felt the proverbial "lively sense of future favors." Jargeau, Meung, Beaugency, were still in English hands; from these sentinel towns up and down the Loire the enemy kept strict watch over Orleans, and there could be no freedom of coming or going. These towns, it appeared, must be taken before the cry 'To Paris!' could be raised in good earnest.

Very well! let them be taken, said the Maid; Jargeau first, then the others On June 11th[1] she and Alençon set forth, with about three thousand troops and a large following of citizens and country people. All were eager to follow her banner, to share in her labors and her victory.

Before telling the story of the "Week of Victories," let us see what her brothers-in-arms, the knightly captains of France, thought of the Maid of Domrémy. They had fought at her side through an arduous campaign; they were entering, with joyful ardor, on another. Andrew Lang has carefully selected three passages from the mass of contemporaneous evidence;

[1] Lowell Lang calls it June 9th

the judgment of three notable military experts, De Termes, Dunois, and Alençon. De Termes speaks first.

"At the assaults before Orleans, Jeanne showed valor and conduct which no man could excel in war. All the captains were amazed by her courage and energy, and her endurance. . . . In leading and arraying, and in encouraging men, she bore herself like the most skilled captain in the world, who all his life had been trained to war."

Then comes Alençon, her "gentle Duke," with: "She was most expert in war, as much in carrying the lance as in mustering a force and ordering the ranks, and in laying the guns. All marveled how cautiously and with what foresight she went to work, as if she had been a captain with twenty or thirty years of experience."

Finally Dunois says: "She displayed (at Troyes) marvelous energy, doing more work than two or three of the most famous and practised men of the sword could have done."

Lang, summing these things up, concludes that [1] "her skill is a marvel, like that of the

---

[1] Lang, pp 136 and 137

untutored Clive, but nobody knows the limits of the resources of nature."

It is easier to begin upon quotations than to cease from them. I may fitly close this chapter with a passage from Boucher de Molandon:

"All those to whom it has been given to kindle the nations, have cared much less to be in advance of their time than to make use of the exciting elements of the time itself. Such is Jeanne d'Arc, whose merit and power alike it was not to innovate upon, but to draw from her epoch the best that it contained. Skilful above all others in finding happy expressions, the ringing note that roused to action, when she speaks of the blood of France, it is because the word has a meaning for all; she wakes a great echo. She sounds the ancient trumpet blast, and the illustrious dead, from Clovis to Du Guesclin, stir in their tombs, and cause the soil of France to tremble under their discouraged descendants."

CHAPTER XII

THE WEEK OF VICTORIES

ON June 11th, as we have seen, Joan rode forth on her new errand. Beside food and ammunition, grateful Orleans furnished artillery for the expedition. Five sloops, manned by forty boatmen, brought heavy guns and field pieces down the river, while "twenty-four horses were needed to drag the chariot of the huge gun of position, resembling Mons Meg, now in Edinburgh Castle."[1]

Ropes and scaling-ladders, too, were provided; these were easily carried. Thus equipped, the troop marched bravely on, halting only when a short march from the town of Jargeau. The town apparently awaited them with little concern. Its walls were strong, its fosse deep and filled with water. Inside was

[1] Lang, p 138

the Earl of Suffolk with six hundred men, an ample number for defence. He was probably watching at this moment from the church tower, but he made no sign.

A discussion rose among the leaders of the advancing troop. Should they storm the fortress, or proceed by slower methods?

Joan was for the assault. "Success is certain," she said. "If I had not assurance of this from God, I would rather herd sheep than put myself in so great jeopardy."

She started on, and the others followed. Now a gate opened in the wall: a band of English rode out, and attacking the French skirmishers, drove them back. Thereupon the Maid seized the standard, rallied her men, repulsed the sally, and took possession of the suburbs of the town. So far, so good! Next morning the guns opened fire on both sides, and banged away merrily for some time, one of those from Orleans, *La Bergère*, demolishing one of the towers in the wall. Here seemed to be a practicable breach ready for the storming. A council was hastily called. The Maid, Alençon, Dunois, Xaintrailles—where was La Hire? Someone had heard that La

Hire was at the moment holding a parley with the English commander. Sent for in haste (and in some heat, be it said; "I and the other leaders were ill content with La Hire!" says Alençon), he appeared with the tidings that Suffolk offered to surrender if no relief came within fifteen days.

Joan had summoned the enemy the night before, and was quite clear in her mind. If the English would depart in their tunics, without arms or armor, they might do so; otherwise the town should be stormed. The other leaders decided that the English might take their horses as well as doublets. Sir John Fastolf was coming from Paris, and it would be well to be off with the old foe before they were on with the new.

Suffolk, naturally enough, refused these terms. The French heralds sounded the assault.

"Forward, gentle Duke!" cried the Maid. "To the assault!"

Alençon hesitated. Was the breach definitely practicable?

"Doubt not!" cried the Maid. "It is the hour that God has chosen. The good Lord helps those who help themselves. Ah! gentle Duke," she added, with the pretty touch of raillery that was all her own; "are you afraid? Do you not know that I promised your wife to bring you back safe and sound, better than when you left?"

She had her way; the ladders were placed, the French swarmed to the assault, while on both sides the cannon thundered defiance. Watching with Alençon near the breach, Joan suddenly cried, "Stand aside! that gun—" and she pointed toward a certain cannon on the wall—"will slay you!" The Duke stepped aside. A few minutes later the Sieur de Lude, standing on the same spot, was killed by a shot from the gun she had indicated.

This time the Maid could not give warning; she was rushing into the breach, the faithful Duke at her side. Seeing this, Suffolk called out, begging to speak with Alençon; but it was too late. Alençon was already following his leader up a scaling-ladder.

No easy task, climbing a long ladder (for Jargeau walls were high), in plate armor, carrying a heavy standard; but so the Maid went. Part way up a stone struck her, tearing he standard and crushing in the light helmet she wore. She fell, but was up again in an instant.

"On, friends, on! God has judged them. Be of good courage; within an hour they are ours!"

It did not need an hour. In an instant, it seemed to Alençon, the city was taken, its commander captured, its defenders fleeing in disorder. Over a thousand men were slain in the pursuit; Joan and Alençon returned in triumph to Orleans, and once more the town went mad over its glorious Pucelle.

She might well have rested after this, one would think, but no! Two days later, she said to d'Alençon, "To-morrow, after dinner, I wish to pay a visit to the English at Meung. Give orders to the company to march at that hour!"[1]

They marched, came to Meung, took the bridge-head (a strong fortification) by assault, and placed a garrison there, but made no attempt to enter the city. This was a visit, not a capture. They slept in the fields, and next morning were on the march again. Beaugency, the next town, saw them coming, and the Eng-

[1] A Lang, p 141

lish garrison promptly evacuated the town, retiring into the castle, but leaving various parties in ambush here and there in sheds and outbuildings, to surprise the invaders.

The invaders refused to be surprised; planted their cannon, and began a bombardment in regular form. But that evening a singular complication arose. Word came to the two young commanders that Arthur of Richemont, Constable of France, was close at hand, with a large body of troops. Now Charles, or rather La Trémoille, was at daggers drawn with Richemont, and Alençon had received a royal mandate forbidding him to have any dealings with the Constable, who happened to be his own uncle. Here was a quandary! Alençon was loyal to the core; how could he disobey his sovereign? On the other hand he had no quarrel with his uncle, and the latter's help would be invaluable. They slept on their doubts and fears, an anxious and foreboding sleep. In the morning word came that the English army was advancing under Talbot and Fastolf This was the precipitating drop in the cup of trembling. "To arms!" cried the soldiers; and Alençon and the Maid mounted their horses and rode to meet De Richemont.

The Constable also had received a royal mandate. He was forbidden to advance, on pain of high displeasure; if he did so, he would be attacked. Neither the Dauphin nor his followers would have anything to do with him. Richemont, who knew that this message came in reality from La Trémoille, about whom he cared nothing at all, continued to advance; and on the 16th day of June came upon Alençon and the Maid riding to meet him with Dunois, La Hire, and the rest

"Joan," said the bluff Constable, "I was told that you meant to attack me. I know not whether you come from God or not; if you are from God, I fear you not at all, for God knows my good will; if you are from the devil, I fear you still less."

"Ah, fair Constable," said the Maid "You have not come for my sake, but you are welcome!"

So all was well that ended well. The threatening breach was closed, and over it the allied forces rode on to meet the English.

These too had had their troubles. Talbot

and Fastolf had met at Janville and held a council, but could not be of one mind. Fastolf, a cautious man, was for delay. Their men, he said, were disheartened by recent events; the French were in full flush of triumph with the send of victory behind them; best for themselves to stand fast, and keep such strongholds as were still theirs, leaving Beaugency to its fate.

This discreet plan little suited John Talbot. Give way, without battle, to a girl? Not he! though he had only his proper escort and such as elected to follow him, yet, he vowed, with the aid of God and St. George he would fight the French.

The weaker man yielded, albeit protesting to the last moment; the old lion marshaled his troops, and on June 18th at Patay, between Orleans and Châteaudun, rode out to battle.

It was evening of the 17th when the French, arrayed in order of battle on a little hill, *"une petite montagnette,"* saw their enemy advancing across a wide plain. Beholding them Joan the Maid cried to those beside her, "They are ours! if they were hung from the clouds above me, we must have them!"

On came the valiant English, and ranged themselves in battle array at the foot of the little hill. Talbot knew well that the others had the advantage of position. Behoved him to break the line which stood so firm above him. He sent two heralds to say that "there were three knights who would fight the French if they would come down."

The French replied, "The hour is late: go to your rest for this day. To-morrow, if it be the good pleasure of God and Our Lady, we shall meet at closer quarters!"

The English did not follow this advice, but fell back on Meung, and spent the night in battering the bridge-head towers which the French had taken and were holding. Next morning they would assault and re-take the towers, then march to the relief of Beaugency.

Morning found them collecting doors and other things to shelter them during the storming of the forts; when a pursuivant came in hot haste from Beaugency, announcing that the French had taken town and fort and were now on their way to find the English generals.

Hereupon the said English generals dropped the doors and other things, departed from

Meung, and took the road to Paris, marching in good order across the wide wooded plain of the Beauce. Behind them, but well out of sight, pricked the advancing French.

What followed reads more like 'a child's game than a life and death struggle of brave men. The French were seeking the English, but had no idea of their whereabouts. The Maid, being appealed to, said confidently, "Ride boldly on! You will have good guidance."

To Alençon, who asked her privately what they should do, she replied, "Have good spurs!"

"How? Are we then to turn our backs?"

"Not so! but there will be need to ride boldly; we shall give a good account of the English, and shall need good spurs to follow them."

On the morning of June 18th Joan said, "To-day the gentle king shall have the greatest victory he has yet had."

For some reason—probably because they wished to keep her in a place of safety, fearing ambuscades in this unknown country—Joan did not lead the advance this day. An enemy might lurk behind any clump of oak or beech; they would not risk their precious Maid in so precarious an adventure.

This was not to the Maid's taste; she was very angry, we are told, for she loved to lead the vanguard: however it chanced, La Hire was the fortunate gallant who rode forward, with eighty men of his company, "mounted on the flower of chargers," to find the English and report when found. Briefly, a scouting party.

"So they rode on and they rode on," till at last they saw on their right the spires of Lignerolles, on their left those of Patay, two little cities of the plain, thick set in woods. This was all they saw, for the English, though directly in front of them, were close hidden in thickets and behind hedges.

Talbot himself led the van. Coming to a lane between two tall hedges he dismounted, and, mindful it may be of the moment at Agincourt

> "When from the meadow by,
> Like a storm suddenly,
> The English archery
> Struck the French horses,"

selected five hundred skilled archers, and proceeded to instal them behind the hedges, declaring that he would hold the pass till his main and rear guard came up.

"But another thing befell him!" says the old chronicle.

On came La Hire and his eighty cavaliers, dashing across the open, crashing through the woods, who so merry as they?

Now these woods held other living things beside English archers. At the sound of crackling and rending branches, up sprang a noble stag, startled from his noonday rest, and fled through the forest as if the hounds were at his heels. So fleeing, the frightened creature rushed full into the main body of the English, hurrying to join Talbot. An Englishman is an Englishman, the world over. They did not know the French were near, but I am not sure that it would have made any difference if they had. Clear, loud, and triumphant, every man of them raised the "view halloo," as good sportsmen should. La Hire heard, and checked his horse instantly; sent back a message to Alençon and the Maid, the one word "*Found!*" formed his eighty in order of battle, and charged with such fury down Talbot's lane that the English archers were cut to pieces before they could loose a shaft.

Fastolf now came rushing up to join Talbot, but finding himself too late, drew rein, and suffered himself to be led—somewhat ignominiously, it was thought—from the field; "making the greatest dole that ever man made."

Well might he lament. The battle of Patay was followed by a massacre of the English, which the Maid was powerless to prevent. The French had suffered too long, the iron had entered too deep into their souls. As the world stood then, they would have been more or less than human to have held their hand from the slaughter. It seemed probable that Joan did not see all of the butchery, but she saw more than enough. "She was most pitiful," says the page d'Aulon, "at the sight of so great a slaughter. A Frenchman was leading some English prisoners; he struck one of them on the head; the man fell senseless. Joan sprang from her saddle and held the Englishman's head in her lap, comforting him; and he was shriven." [1]

Talbot was taken by Xaintrailles, and led

[1] Translated by Andrew Lang

by him before Alençon, the Maid and de Richemont.

"You did not look for this in the morning, Lord Talbot!" said Alençon, who had been a prisoner in England.

"It is the fortune of war!" said the old lion; and no other word of his is recorded.

The Week of Victories was over, and once more Joan returned to her Orleans, to joy-bells and masses, adoring crowds and friendly hearthstones. This time she found a present awaiting her at the house of *Père* Boucher, a present at once quaint and pathetic

Fourteen years had passed since Agincourt was lost and won, and Charles of Orleans was still a prisoner in England, still writing poetry like his fellow-prisoner and poet, James I. of Scotland. He had heard of the grievous peril of his city, and of its glorious rescue by the wonder-working Maid. He would fain show his gratitude in some seemly and appropriate way. Therefore, "considering the good and agreeable service of the Pucelle against the English, ancient enemies of the King and himself," he ordered the treasurer (of Orleans) to offer in his name to the young heroine a suit—

of armor?—By no means! a costume of state, *"vêtement d'apparat,"* such as gentlewomen wore. The colors of his house were to be used; "a robe of fine scarlet cloth, with a tunic (*huque*) of dark green stuff." "A tailor of renown" was charged with the making of the costume; the items of expense have been preserved.

Two ells of scarlet cloth cost eight gold crowns; the lining, two crowns more One ell of green stuff, two crowns. For making a robe and *huque*, with trimming of white satin, sendal, and other stuff, one crown. Total, thirteen gold crowns, equal to about twenty dollars of our money. Not an extravagant present, you say, in return for a royal city. But Joan had looked for no reward, and Charles gave what he could. Be sure that the Maid was well pleased with her costume of state; I cannot repeat too often that she was seventeen, and fair as a white rose. She may even have worn it—who knows? during those few days of rest, after Patay, at Père Boucher's. She loved pretty clothes. One can fancy the astonishment of Alençon, coming clanking in his armor to take counsel with his fellow-commander, to find her blushing rose-like in scarlet and green. It is a pretty picture. Those were the days of the hennin, but I cannot think that the Maid ever, even for a moment, crowned her short dark locks with that most hideous invention of fashion. We all know it in pictures; the single or double-horned headdress (I know not which is uglier!) often reaching monstrous proportions, with which the fashionable women of that day were infatuated. The single hennin was often two or three feet in height; the double one perhaps nearly as wide.

In the first year of the siege of Orleans one Friar Thomas preached a crusade against the extravagance of women's dress, and especially against the hennin. "He was so vehement against them," says Monstrelêt, "that no woman thus dressed dared to appear in his presence, for he was accustomed when he saw any with such dresses, to excite the little boys to torment and plague them. He ordered the boys to shout after them, *'Au hennin! au hennin!'* even when the ladies were departed from him, and from hearing his invectives; and the boys pursuing them endeavored to pull down these monstrous head-dresses, so that the ladies were forced to seek shelter in places of safety. These cries caused many tumults between those who raised them and the servants of the ladies. For a time the ladies were ashamed, and came to mass in close caps, 'such as those of nuns.' But this reform lasted not, for like as snails, when anyone passes them, draw in their horns, and when all danger seems over, put them forth again—so these ladies, shortly after the preacher had quitted their country, forgetful of his doctrine and abuse, began to resume their former colossal head-dresses, and wore them even higher than before."

A terrible fellow, this Friar Thomas. Monstrelêt further tells us that "at sermons he divided women from men by a cord, having observed some sly doings between them while he was preaching."

Sometimes, after an eloquent sermon on the pains of hell and damnation, he would summon his hearers to bring him all games and toys; all hennins and other abominations of dress; and having a fire ready burning, would throw

these vanities in and make an end of them for
that time.

Here is a long digression about hennins, as
I say, I do not believe Joan ever put one on
her head; nor did Friar Thomas, so far as I
know, ever come to Orleans.

.

CHAPTER XIII

RHEIMS

THINGS began to look worse and worse for La Trémoille "By reason of Joan the Maid," says the old chronicle, "so many folks came from all parts unto the king for to serve him at their own charges, that La Trémoille and others of the council were full wroth thereat, through anxiety for their own persons"

That figure of a united France, which shone so bright and gracious before the eyes of the Maid, was to La Trémoille and his minions a spectre of doom. They put forth all their forces of inertia and procrastination—mighty forces indeed when skilfully handled—and spun their cobwebs of intrigue close and closer about the foolish Dauphin.

Rejoicing Orleans thought her prince would come to share her triumph, and through her gates would ride forth to that coronation which was to consummate and render stable the glorious victories of the past weeks. They adorned their streets, hung out their richest tapestries for the royal visitor; but Charles was visiting La Trémoïlle at the latter's castle of Sully, and made no movement. Joan waited a day or two, and then took horse and rode to Sully. She had no time to waste, however it might be with others. Earnestly and reverently she besought Charles to make no more delay, but ride with her at once to Rheims for his coronation.

Charles regretted the severity of the Maid's labors; was very pleased at the victories; thought she ought to take a holiday; shortly, no one knows why, left Sully and went to Châteauneuf, fifteen miles down the river. Joan followed him, and again made her prayer. She wept as she knelt before him. The cruel toil, the bloodshed and the glory—was all to be for naught? The days were flying, every day bringing her nearer the end. The Dauphin, moved by her tears, bade her dry her eyes, all would be well.

But while Charles dawdled and La Trémoille shuffled his cards and spun his webs,
France was rising. The news of Orleans and
Patay flew on the wings of the wind, birds of
the air carried it.

In La Rochelle the bells were rung; Te
Deum was sung; bonfires blazed, and every
child was given a cake to run and shout
"Noel!" before the triumphal procession. The
name of the Maid was on every lip, every heart
beat high for her. Knowing this, as she must
have known it, small wonder that she chafed
and wept at the delay

She rode to Gien, where long and weary
councils were held, and ten more precious days
wasted. Here people came flocking from all
parts of the realm, to join her standard, for
love of her and of France. The royal
treasury was empty; no matter for that!
Gentlemen who were too poor to equip themselves properly came armed with bows and
arrows, with hunting knives, with anything that
could cut or pierce. One gallant soldier,
"Bueil, one of the French leaders," stole linen
from the drying-lines of a neighboring castle
to make himself decent to appear at court.

"Each one of them," says the old chronicle, "had firm belief that through Joan much good would come to the land of France, and so they longed greatly to serve her, and learned of her deeds as if they were God's own."

Miracle and portent sprang up to aid the cause. In Poitou knights in blazing armor were seen riding down the sky, and it was clear that they threatened ruin to the Duke of Brittany, who still favored the English.

The joints of the favorite were loosened, and his knees smote together; yet at this time none dared speak openly against him, though all knew that it was he who blocked the way. But for him, men said, the French might now be strong enough to sweep the English finally and completely from their soil.

John of Bedford, in Paris, trying his best to rule France, since that was the task that had been set him, wrote to his young master in England:

"All things here prospered for you till the time of the siege of Orleans, undertaken by whose advice God only knows. Since the death of my cousin of Salisbury, whom God absolve, who fell by the hand of God, as it seemeth, your people, who were assembled in great number at this siege, have received a terrible check. This has been caused in part, as we trow, by the confidence our enemies have in a disciple and limb of the devil, called Pucelle, that used false enchantments and sorcery. The which stroke and discomfiture has not only lessened the number of your people here, but also sunk the courage of the remainder in a wonderful manner, and encouraged your enemies to assemble themselves forthwith in great numbers."[1]

The enemies of England were not all encouraged. There were others besides La Trémoille at the councils of Gien who advised against the ride to Rheims. The way was long, and thick set with strong places garrisoned by English and Burgundians. There would be great danger for the Dauphin and all concerned

"I know all that, and care nothing for it!" cried the Maid; and in desperation she rode out of the town and bivouacked in the open fields, her faithful comrades about her.

Deep as was her distress, her determination

[1] "Pictorial History of England," Knight, p 88.

never wavered. She wrote to the people of Tournai, who had been faithful throughout to the Dauphin's cause, "Loyal Frenchmen, I pray and require you to be ready to come to the coronation of the gentle King Charles at Rheims, where we shall shortly be, and to come and meet us so soon as ye shall learn of our approach."

This was on June 25th; on the 29th, La Trémoille and the Dauphin yielded reluctantly enough to the irresistible force of public enthusiasm. The Maid had already started. The stage was set for the coronation; there was really no help for it.

So off they set for Rheims, Dauphin, favorite, court and all, following the Maid of Domrémy.

It was no holiday procession. As had been foreseen, there were obstacles, and plenty of them. Auxerre would not open its gates; sent, it was said, a bribe of two thousand crowns to save itself from assault; but sent also food (at a price!) to the advancing army.

Troyes, a little farther on, had sworn allegiance to England and Burgundy. Coronation at Rheims? The Trojans knew nothing about it. They had a garrison, English and Burgundian, five or six thousand good stout men; they snapped their fingers at Maid and Dauphin; would not hear of admitting them. Had not Brother Richard, the Cordelier friar, warned them against this Maid, saying that she was, or might be, a female Antichrist? Had he not bidden them sow beans in vast quantities in case of emergency?

Here were the beans, whole fields of them, in evidence! here was also Brother Richard himself, breathing forth fire and fury. Presently the holy brother, who seems to have been a second edition of Father Thomas, preaching repentance and practicing the destruction of vanities, came forth to exorcise the Maid; threw holy water at her, and made the sign of the cross. Joan laughed her pleasant, merry laugh; bade him take courage and come forward. She would not fly away, she assured him. Whereupon, at nearer view of the supposed sorceress and limb of evil, Brother Richard suffered a sudden change of heart; perceived that here was a thing divine; plumped down on his knees to do homage: but the good Maid knelt too, humbly, in token that she was "of like passions" with himself. Soon the pair were good friends, and the friar hurried back to the city and declared that the Maid was of God, and could if she wished fly over the walls.

Troyes heard, but kept its gates shut. Anxious council was held in the Dauphin's camp; La Trémoille advised retreat; had he not said all along, etc., etc.

The archbishop of Rheims, chancellor of France and a tool of La Trémoille, drew lurid pictures of the strength of Troyes and the contumaciousness of its people. They never would yield; the supplies of the army were running low. Best retire while they could do so with safety. The councillors were called on in turn for their opinion; some advised retreating, some passing by the obstinate town in hope of faring better elsewhere; hardly one favored an attack on the city.

When the turn came of Robert de Maçon, sometime chancellor (of Charles VI.), he said bluntly, "This march was begun not because we were rich in money or strong in men, but because Joan the Maid said it was the will of God. Let the Maid be summoned, and let the Council hear what she has to say on the matter!"

Joan was sent for, and was told the sense of the meeting; the lions in the path; the necessity of retreat.

To the Archbishop, who addressed her, she made no reply, but turned to her prince. "Do you believe all this, gentle Dauphin?" she asked.

Charles was not sure, perhaps, what La Trémoille would allow him to believe. He made cautious answer; if the Maid had anything profitable and reasonable to say, she would be trusted.

"Good Dauphin," said the Maid in her clear thrilling voice, "command your people to advance to the siege, and waste no more time in councils; in God's name, before three days pass I will bring you into Troyes, by favor or force or valor, and false Burgundy shall be greatly amazed."

Even the Archbishop seems to have been impressed by these words.

"Joan," he said, "we could wait for six days were we sure of having the town, but can we be sure?"

"Have no doubt of it!" replied the Maid. Thereupon she mounted her horse and rode through the camp, banner in hand, exhorting, encouraging, ordering preparations for the assault.

Following the example of the English at Meung, she collected doors, tables, screens, to shelter the advance, bundles of fagots to fill in the ditches.

"Immediately," says Dunois (*quorum pars magna,* we may well believe), "she crossed the river with the royal army and pitched tents close by the wall, laboring with a diligence that not two or three most experienced and renowned captains could have shown."

All night she worked, never pausing for an hour. When morning broke, the burgesses of Troyes, looking over their battlements, saw an army in storming array; saw in the very front a slender figure in white armor, waving on her men.

"To the assault!" cried the Maid; and made a sign to fill the ditch with fagots. At the sight the hearts of the men of Troyes turned to water. They sent their Bishop to make terms, and the city opened its gates to the Dauphin and the Maid.

Four days later the Bishop of Chalôns appeared with the keys of his city, which the little Army of Triumph entered July 14th. At Chalôns Joan found several men of Domrémy, who had come from the village to see the glory of their own Maid. To one of them, her godfather, she gave a red cap—or some say a robe—that she had worn; she was full of kindly and neighborly words; told one of them who had been Burgundian in his sympathies that she feared nothing but treachery. About this time she said to the king, in Alençon's hearing, "Make good use of my time! I shall hardly last longer than a year."

Two days after this, halting at Sept-Saule, the Dauphin received a deputation from Rheims. The holy city had been strongly Anglo-Burgundian till now; had vowed unshakable loyalty to John of Bedford and Philip of Burgundy. But this was while Troyes still held out; Troyes, which had "sworn on the precious body of Jesus Christ to resist to the death." Now, Troyes had submitted, and her people wrote to those of Rheims begging them to do likewise, assuring them that the Dauphin was everything that was lovely and of good report; moreover, *"une belle personne!"* Their own Archbishop wrote too, charging them to make submission to their lawful prince. What was a holy city to do?

"Bow thy head meekly, O Sicambrian! adore——" was St. Remy speaking again in the person of this peasant maid? Must the city of Clovis bow like him, taking on new vows and forswearing old?

There seemed no help for it. Accordingly the deputation was sent, inviting Charles to enter his loyal city of Rheims; and people began to make ready for the coronation.

Rheims; Durocortorum of the Romans; an important town in the days of Caesar, faithful to him and to his followers, and receiving special favors in recognition of its fidelity.

The Vandals captured it in 406, and slew St. Nicasus; later, Attila and his Huns visited it with fire and sword. Later still, as we know, it saw the baptism of Clovis, and became the Holy City of France, where all her kings would fain be crowned. Did not men say that the phial of oil used in that kingly baptism by St.

Remy, and still preserved in his abbey, was brought to him by a white dove, straight from heaven? Accordingly the kings were crowned there, from Philip Augustus in 1180 to Charles X. in 1824.

Now, on the seventeenth day of July, 1429, Charles of Valois, seventh of that name, was to receive his solemn sacring, and to become king of France *de jure*, if not yet *de facto*. The ceremony began at nine in the morning.

"A right fair thing it was," wrote Pierre de Beauvais to the queen, "to see that fair mystery, for it was as solemn and as well adorned with all things thereto pertaining, as if it had been ordered a year before." [1]

First, a company of knights and nobles in full armor, headed by the Maréchal de Boursac, rode out to meet the Abbot of St. Rémy, who came from his abbey bringing the holy phial (*ampoule*). Then they all rode into the cathedral, and alighted at the choir-gate. There met them Charles the Dauphin, and presently received his consecration at the hands of the Archbishop, and was anointed and crowned king of France. The people shouted

[1] Trans. A. Lang.

"*Noël!*" and blessed God for the auspicious day.

"And the trumpets sounded so that you might think the roofs would be rent. And always during that mystery the Maid stood next the King, her standard in her hand. A right fair thing it was to see the goodly manners of the King and the Maid." [1]

D'Albert carried the Sword of State; Alençon gave the accolade Guy de Laval was there, and La Trémoille, and many others whose names we know; all in their brightest armor, we may be sure, with much clanking of swords and waving of banners. We hardly see them; all our eyes are for the Maid (she also in full armor, as becomes a good soldier), as she kneels before the King she has made, embracing his knees and weeping for joy.

"Gentle King," she says, "now is accomplished the Will of God, who decreed that I should raise the siege of Orleans and bring you to this city of Rheims to receive your solemn sacring, thereby showing that you are the true king, and that France shall be yours."

The chronicle adds, "And right great pity came upon all who saw her, and many wept."

[1] Trans A Lang

If this might have been the end! if she might have turned now, in the hour of her triumph, her task accomplished, and the bidding of her Voices done—have turned away from the warfare and the pomp, the cabals and the intrigues, and gone back to Domrémy, to tend her sheep and mind her spinning-wheel, and dream over "the great days done!"

Tradition has long held that this was the wish of her heart, and that after the coronation she begged Charles to let her depart in peace, now that her mission was ended. This legend seems to have no foundation in fact; it probably sprang from the universal feeling; "Might it have been!" We shall see, however, that somewhat later she expressed to others her desire to depart. The relief of Orleans and the coronation of the king were all, says Dunois, that she actually claimed as her mission; beyond this all was vague. Still, the Voices said that the English must be driven from French soil, and Joan was the last one to take her hand from the plough while work was still to do. Forward then, in God's name, since thus it must be!

I have never seen Rheims Cathedral, and

now I shall never see it with my bodily eyes; yet to me, as to all of this day and generation, it is intimately familiar in both its aspects. First we see it the crown and glory of Gothic architecture, the "frozen music," the "rugged lacework" whose praises men have sung for seven hundred years, yet whose beauty has never been expressed in words.

Next we see it—every child knows how. Let us not dwell upon it. One thought brightens against the dark background of ruin and desolation. Through all the four-years' agony of Rheims, while this sacred Heart of her was crashing and splintering under the deadly shell-fire; while the splendors of its great rose-window were tinkling in rainbow showers down on its uptorn pavements; while the very lead from its roofs was dripping down in those curious lengths and festoons of clinging particles which men now call "the tears of Rheims," one thing remained untouched. Before the Cathedral (which with its ruined and dying body seemed to shelter her), quiet through the thunders of the bombardment, marble on her marble steed, still sat the Maid of France.

CHAPTER XIV

PARIS

CHARLES of Valois was king of France
The first of Joan's appointed tasks
was fulfilled, and with clear faith and resolve
she turned to the second. The English must
be driven from the soil of France. To this
end, the word was "Paris!" and on Paris,
might the Maid have her way, the king's
conquering army should march forthwith.

She and Alençon had thought to set out
the day after the coronation; but on the very
day of the ceremony, July 17th, came to
Rheims an embassy from Philip Duke of Burgundy, asking for a truce.

Joan greatly desired peace with Burgundy,
knowing that there could be no lasting victory
without it. She had written to the Duke a
month before this, but had received no reply:
now, on July 17th, she wrote again in her
simple direct fashion.

"High and mighty prince, duke of Burgundy, I, Joan the Maid, in the name of the King of Heaven, my rightful and sovereign Lord, bid you and the king of France make a good, firm peace, which shall endure. Do each of you pardon the other, heartily and wholly, as loyal Christians should, and, if you like to fight, go against the Saracens. Prince of Burgundy, I pray and beseech and beg you as humbly as I may, that you war no more on the holy kingdom of France, but at once cause your people who are in any places and fortresses of this holy kingdom to withdraw; and as for the gentle king of France, he is ready to make peace with you if you are willing, saving his honor; and I bid you know, in the name of the King of Heaven, my rightful and sovereign Lord, for your well-being and your honor and on your life, that you will never gain a battle against loyal Frenchmen; and that all who war in the holy kingdom of France war against King Jesus, King of Heaven and all the earth, my rightful and sovereign Lord. With folded hands I pray and beg you to fight no battle and wage no war against us, neither you, your soldiers, nor your people, for what-

ever number of soldiers you bring against us,
know of a surety that they shall gain nothing,
but it will be a great pity to see the great battle
and the blood which will flow from those who
come there against us. Three weeks ago I
wrote and sent you good letters by a herald,
bidding you to the king's consecration, which
takes place to-day, Sunday, the seventeenth of
this present month of July, in the city of
Rheims, but I have had no answer, and have
heard no news of the herald. To God I com-
mend you, and may He keep you, if it please
Him, and I pray God to bring about a good
peace "[1]

The very day after came the Burgundian
envoys, with peace on their lips Joan could
not know that a few days before, while she
and Charles were before Troyes, Philip of
Burgundy had entered Paris in person, and
standing beside John of Bedford had proclaimed his wrongs, telling again the oft-told
tale of his father's murder, and calling on the
people of Paris to swear allegiance to himself
and Bedford. Having done this, he dispatched
his embassy to beguile Charles into a truce,

which should give him and the English time
to make further preparations.

Charles was always ready to be beguiled.
For the moment, however, the tide of triumph
and devotion was too strong for him. He was
carried hither and thither by it; to the abbey of
St. Macoul, where he "touched" for the King's
Evil; to Soissons, the keys of which had been
sent him in due submission. Everywhere he
was received with joyful acclamations; everywhere the Maid rode before him, in the
knight's or page's dress which she affected
when not in armor, trunks and short coat of
rich materials, well furred. What had become
of the scarlet and green Orleans costume we do
not know; in any case she could not have worn
it on horseback.

The way lay clear before them to Paris, only
sixty miles distant. One might think that even
Charles VII. might have heard the Brazen
Head of the fable speak loud and clear: *"Time
is!"*

But Charles was listening to the men of
Burgundy, and dawdling, which after all was
the occupation he loved best. He spent four
or five precious days at Soissons, then dawdled

across the Marne to Château Thierry, where
six hundred years later Yankee boys were to
defend gloriously that soil of France which he
betrayed and insulted. At Château Thierry he
at least did one thing. On the last day of July
"in favor and at the request of our beloved Joan
the Maid, considering the great, high, notable
and profitable service which she has rendered
and doth daily render us in the recovery of our
kingdom," the king declared the villages of
Domrémy and Greux free from taxes forever.
Through nearly three hundred years the tax-
gatherer's book bore these words, written
against the names of these two villages: *"Nothing; for the Maid."* In the reign of Louis
XV. this freedom, with many others, came to
an end.

As Charles loitered about the neighborhood,
as contemptible a figure as History can show
in all her ample page, the delighted people still
flocked from neighboring towns and villages to
do homage to him and the Maid. Joan loved
these plain country folk with their joyous greetings. "What good devout people these are!"
she exclaimed one day, as she rode between
Dunois and the archbishop of Rheims. "Never

have I seen any people who so greatly rejoiced over the coming of a king so noble. When I come to die, I would well that it might be in these parts."

"Joan," said the archbishop, "is it known to you when you will die, and at what place?"

Dunois, who rode at her bridle rein, reports her answer.

"Where it shall please God! Of the hour and the place I know no more than you. I have done that which my Lord commanded me, to deliver Orleans and have the gentle king crowned. Would that it might please God my Creator to suffer me to depart at this time and lay down my arms, and go to serve my father and mother in keeping their sheep, with my sisters and brothers, who would be right glad to see me."

And all the people shall say Amen!

Was the good Maid beginning to have glimpses of the clay feet of her idol? If so, she gave no sign. Her loyalty never wavered for an instant, but she was bewildered—how should she not have been?—at the result of her shining deeds. She had laid a kingdom at Charles's feet; he let it lie there, and drifted

PARIS

from place to place, dragging her with him.
On August 5th she wrote a pathetic letter to
the people of Rheims, doing her poor best to
reassure them, who saw their new crowned king
apparently deserting them.

"Dear and good friends," she says, "good
and loyal Frenchmen, the Maid sends you her
greetings"; and goes on to assure them that she
will never abandon them while she lives.
"True it is that the King has made a fifteen
days' truce with the Duke of Burgundy, who
is to give up to him the town of Paris on the
fifteenth day. Although the truce is made, I
am not content, and am not certain that I will
keep it. If I do, it will be merely for the sake
of the King's honor, and in case they do not
deceive the blood royal, for, I will keep the
King's army together and in readiness, at the
end of the fifteen days, if peace is not made." [2]

Finally she bade the people trust her, and
be of good heart—striving, poor soul, to lift
their hearts, while her own was sinking daily
—and to warn her if traitors should be found
among them.

John of Bedford, one may think, was no

[1] Translated by Andrew Lang

less puzzled than the Maid. He too saw the
kingdom at those loitering, shambling feet;
but he was not the man to wait the pleasure
of the shambler. He sent to England for five
thousand stout men-at-arms, and established
them in Paris. One division of this army bore
a standard, in the centre of which appeared a
distaff filled with cotton, with a half-filled
spindle hanging to it. The field was set with
empty spindles, and inscribed with the legend:
"Now, fair one, come!"

At the same time Bedford sent a letter to
Charles from Montereau, beginning, "You
formerly self-styled Dauphin, and now calling
yourself King," charging him with receiving
help from an abandoned and dissolute woman,
wearing men's apparel, and an apostate and
seditious Friar; "both, according to Holy
Scripture, things abominable to God." The
duke begged the king to have pity on the
unhappy people of France, and to meet him at
some convenient place, where terms of peace
might be discussed. It should be a true peace,
not like that once made by Charles at this
very Montereau, just before he treacherously
slew the duke of Burgundy. Finally, Bedford

challenged Charles to single combat (for which probably no man in France, unless it were La Trémoille, had less stomach) and appealed to the Almighty, who then as now was claimed as bosom friend by all would-be autocrats. Having dispatched this letter, which he hoped would sting Charles into action of some sort, John of Bedford went back to Paris, and set his army in battle array before the closed gates of the city.

Ever since the relief of Orleans, the English had not ceased to assure Joan as occasion served, that whenever and wherever they could lay hands on her they would burn her. The Maid was only too eager to give them their chance.

"I cry, 'Go against the English!'" she exclaimed.

At last, after endless "to-ing and fro-ing," Joan and Alençon took matters into their own hands, and started for Paris, leaving the king to follow as he might. On August 14th they encountered Bedford at Montépilloy, strongly intrenched, in an excellent position. The French advanced to within two bowshots, and boldly defied him to battle. But Bedford had no idea of giving them battle; forbade any general sortie—but, on the French knights' advancing to the very walls, shouting defiance —allowed a little genteel skirmishing here and there. The Maid herself, when she saw that the foe would not come out, "rode to the front, standard in hand and smote the English palisade." Nothing came of it, except a few more skirmishes. Next day the French retreated, thinking to draw their enemy out in pursuit; whereupon the wily Bedford turned about and went back to Paris, "having faced without disaster a superior French force, having encouraged his own troops, and shaken the popular faith in Joan." [1]

Finding the English gone, Joan, Alençon, and Charles went to Compiègne, which had recently sent in its submission, as had Beauvais and Senlis.

Compiègne received its precious king with apparent enthusiasm. With these three towns secure, Joan's spirit rose again for a moment. Now, at last, the way lay open. Forward to Paris, while time still was!

[1] Lowell, pp 168 and 169

Charles found Compiègne a pleasant place, and saw no hurry; was busy, moreover, coquetting again with Burgundy.

"The Maid was in grief," says the chronicle, "for the King's long tarrying at Compiègne; and it seemed he was content, as was his wont, with such grace as God had granted him, and would seek no further adventure." Once more the Maid set out with her faithful army, this time really for Paris, halting not till she reached St. Denis. No sooner was her back turned than Charles and La Trémoille concluded a general truce, to begin at once, August 28th, and to last till Christmas. The English might benefit by it whenever they wished; while it lasted, no more cities might submit to Charles, however much they might wish to do so. The Peace Party had triumphed for the moment.

Meanwhile the Maid was at the gates of Paris; with the king's permission, let us remember!

He allowed her to attack the city, practically at the same moment when he agreed to recognize Burgundy as holding it against her.

Who shall read this riddle? The "Campaign of Dupes," as it has been called, has puzzled historians from that day to this. For us, it is perhaps enough to remember the inheritance of this wretched mortal, child of a mad father and a bad mother. He had already signed the pact with Burgundy when Alençon, after repeated efforts, finally succeeded in dislodging him from his perch at Senlis, and dragged him as far as St. Denis. Here he would be safe, and his near presence would hearten the troops. So thought Joan and Alençon, and so it proved for the moment. There was great rejoicing. "She will put the king in Paris," people said, "if he will let her!" and the men of Orleans and Patay rode about and about the city, examining the fortifications, seeking the best place for an assault, and sending inflammatory messages to their friends inside the walls, those who had once thrilled to the cry of "Armagnac!" and who were now ready to rally to the white standard of the Maid.

September 8th was the Festival of the birth of St. Mary the Virgin. As a rule, Joan did not like to fight on holy days; but the captains were eager to attack, her Voices did not for-

bid, her military instinct bade her strike. At
eight in the morning, she, with old de Gaucourt and Gilles de Rais, advanced against the
gate of St. Honoré, while Alençon with the
reserve forces remained on guard in case of
a possible sortie.

There are many accounts of this attack. A
curious one is that of the *Bourgeois de Paris,*
whose *Journal* throws so vivid a light on these
wild times. The Bourgeois was an ardent
Burgundian, and had no good to say of anything connected with the Armagnacs or their
successors.

"Les Armenalx," he still calls the royal
army; and tells how it appeared before Paris
with "a creature in the form of a woman,
whom they called the Maid." "They came,"
he said, "about the hour of High Mass, between eleven and twelve, their Pucelle with
them, and great store of chariots, carts, and
horses, all loaded with huge fagots to fill the
fosses of Paris, and began to assault between
the gate of St. Honoré and the gate St. Denis,
and the assault was very cruel; and in attacking they said many ill words to those of Paris.
And there was their Pucelle with her standard

on the edge of the fosse crying to those of Paris, 'Yield you in the name of Jesus, to us, and that quickly, for if you do not yield before night, we shall enter by force, will you nill you, and all shall be put to death without mercy.' "

These last words do not ring true; we know that Joan was always for sparing life when it was possible. Another Anglo-Burgundian, Clément de Fauquembergen, describes how the people, at news of the attack, fled from the churches, where they were at prayers, and hid in their cellars; while the defenders of the city took their stations on the walls and made valiant defence, giving the assailants back shot for shot, bolt for bolt.

The first ditch was deep but dry, the second filled with water. Those watching from the walls saw a slender white-clad figure spring forward from the French ranks, lance in hand, saw it climb slowly and carefully down and up the steep sides of the dry ditch, and stand on the brink of the moat.

"The Maid! the Witch of Armagnac!" the murmur ran like flame along the walls, and archers and gunners sprang to their posts and took careful aim at the shining figure.

Serene, unmoved, amid a storm of bullets and arrows, the Maid stood beside the water, probing its black depth with her lance; calling on her men to follow her. So she stands for all time, one of the imperishable pictures.

Another moment, and a bolt from an arblast struck her down. Still, as she lay bleeding from a wound in the thigh, she ceased not to cheer the French on to the assault. Let them only fill the ditch, she cried, and all would be well; the city would be theirs.

It was not to be. The garrison, seeing her fall, redoubled their volleys of iron and stone; the assailants were weary, twilight was gathering, and no radiant armor shone through the dusk to light them on. Now it was night, and all but the Maid knew that the end had come. She, lying beside the ditch, refusing to be moved, still cried for the charge, still gave assurance of victory. At last, long after nightfall, Alençon and de Gaucourt, unable to prevail upon her otherwise, lifted her out of the fosse, set her on a horse, and rode back to the line.

"*Par mon martin,*" she still cried, "the place would have been taken!"

One at least of the Burgundian chroniclers is of her mind. "Had anyone in the king's command," he says, "been as manly as Joan, Paris would have been in danger of capture; but none of the others could agree upon the matter."

Next morning, Friday the ninth, the Maid sent for Alençon and implored him to sound the trumpets and lead the assault. She would never leave the spot, she vowed, till the city was taken. Alençon was willing enough, and some of the captains with him; others demurred. While they debated the matter, came messengers from the king, with orders for them to return at once to St. Denis. La Trémoille had won, and Paris was lost.

Sick at heart, the wounded Maid, with faithful Alençon beside her, rode back, to find Charles busy with plans for retreat. Even Joan must now, one would think, have realized that all was over; yet the two comrades made one last gallant effort. The south wall of Paris might be less strong than that near the gate of St. Honoré. Alençon had already built a bridge across the Seine near St. Denis; how if they crossed this bridge with a chosen few and surprised the town?

Early next morning they rode forth on their perilous venture—to find the bridge destroyed by order of the king

Now indeed Joan tasted the bitterness of defeat. She spoke no word, but her action spoke for her. She hung up her armor before the statue of the Virgin Mother in the cathedral.

Her Voices bade her stay in St. Denis, but for once she must disobey them, obedience not being in her power. Three days later Charles left the place, dragging his followers with him. A hasty march back to the Loire, and on September 21st the king dined at Gien, well out of the way of English and Burgundians.

"And thus," says the chronicle, "were broken the will of the Maid and the army of the king."

.

CHAPTER XV

COMPIÈGNE

A T Gien, the little old town where Charlemagne's castle frowned down upon the peaceful Loire, was bitter wrangling in the days that followed. La Trémoille had got his truce, and meant to enjoy it; Alençon's lance was still in rest, he demanded another campaign, in Normandy this time, and the Maid to lead it with him. Joan, with unerring glance, saw the thing that should be done Let her go to the Isle of France, and from that spot of vantage cut off the supplies of Paris as they came down the river, and so reduce the city! Both these requests were put by. La Trémoille did not mean that Alençon and the Maid should ever fight side by side again. He had his way; the fiery duke, deprived of his command, left the court in anger, and retired to his estate. No sooner was he gone, than Charles disbanded the army, and fell to his dawdling again. Once more the Brazen Head had spoken: *"Time was!"*

Hither and yon he drifted, a dead leaf skipping before the wind; with him, would she or no, went the Maid. Her bright arms were dimmed now by defeat, but still she was valuable—and dangerous! Charles was not yet ready to give her up; La Trémoille did not dare to let her go; she drifted with the rest. At Selles the queen met her precious spouse, and together they drifted to Bourges. Here Joan was lodged in the house of Marguerite La Touroulde, a gentlewoman of the queen's train, and stayed there some weeks, praying often in the churches, giving to the poor, bearing herself, as ever, simply and modestly. Girls brought her their rosaries, begging her to touch them. "Touch them yourselves!" she said laughing. "They will get as much good from your touch as from mine."

She talked much with her kindly hostess, as they sat together in the house, or went to and from mass and confession. Dame Margaret suggested that probably Joan's courage in battle came from the knowledge that she would not be killed.

"I have no such knowledge," said the Maid; "no more than anybody else."

This good woman testified later that Joan gave freely to the poor and with a glad heart, saying, "I am sent for the comfort of the poor and needy." Testified also that the Maid was "very simple and innocent, knowing almost nothing except in affairs of war."[1]

Meantime, Charles and La Trémoille were holding councils, after their manner. What to do, with affairs in general, with the Maid in particular? They must not stir up Burgundy; it would be well to let the English alone just now, while the truce held; yet here was this little saintly firebrand, demanding persistently to be allowed to save the kingdom! Who wanted to save the kingdom? Certainly not La Trémoille. At last, after much cogitation, he hit on a project, at once safe and promising. Here were two little river towns, La Charité and St. Pierre le Moustier, conveniently near by, held for Burgundy by two soldiers of fortune, Perrinet Grasset (who began life a mason), and Francis of Surienne, a Spaniard, uncle of that Rodrigo Borgia who was later

[1] Lang, p 190.

to disedify Christendom as Pope Alexander
VI. La Trémoille had a grudge against
Grasset; had been captured by him once upon
a time, and made to pay a large ransom, to his
great inconvenience. Why not get up an expedition against these two places, and send the
Maid in charge? If she succeeded, well; if
not—still well enough! She would be dis-
credited, and little harm done. They did not
actually need La Charité and St. Pierre le
Moustier, though they would be handy possessions against possible breaking of the truce.

La Trémoille proposed, Charles and the
Council assented. Joan, poor child, welcomed
any chance for action Late in October she
left Bourges, and with her, as titular commander, Charles of Albret, brother-in-law and
follower of La Trémoille, yet withal a good
soldier, who had fought with her at Patay.

St. Pierre le Moustier stood high on its steep
bluff over the river Allier: a strong little town.
well placed, well fortified, well garrisoned.
Albret and Joan invested it in regular form,
and after a week of bombardment, having
made a practicable breach, orders were given
for an assault. The French advanced gal-

lantly, but could make no head against the fire of the defenders. They wavered, began to fall back. But they had to reckon with the Maid, unwounded this time, and feeling her power come upon her. Standing on the edge of the fosse, as she had stood at Paris, she called upon her men to come forward to the assault. They hesitated; for a few moments she stood there almost alone, with only two or three lances about her, among them probably her two brothers, who never deserted her.[1]

D'Aulon, her faithful squire, had been wounded, and stood at a little distance, leaning on his crutches and looking on. Seeing, as he thought, all lost for the time being, he managed to get on his horse, and riding up to the Maid, asked why she stood there in peril of her life, instead of retreating with the others.

Raising the visor of her helmet, Joan looked him full in the face. "I am not alone!" she said quietly. "With me are fifty thousand of my own, and I will not leave this spot till the town is taken."

A strange answer; d'Aulon was a literal-

---

[1] They joined her probably at Orleans; little more is known about them.

minded youth. He looked about him, bewildered. "Whatever she might say," he says in telling the story, "she had only four or five men with her, I know it for certain, and so do several others who looked on; so I urged her to go back with the rest. Then she bade me tell them to bring fagots and fascines to bridge the moat, and she herself in a clear voice gave the same order."

Was it the sight of her? When they failed at Paris, was it because the white-clad figure lay unseen in the fosse, though the brave piteous voice still rang like a trumpet through that twilight of despair? D'Aulon thought it a miracle, as would most people of his time. All in a moment, it seemed, the thing was done; the moat bridged, the troops over it, the town stormed and taken "with no great resistance."

Yet once more, Joan, before your year is over, before your bright day darkens into night! St. John's Day is near.

At La Charité there were no shining deeds; no victory of any sort. For a month the French army lay before the place, and once an assault was attempted; but the weather was bad, the men weary, hungry, dispirited; briefly, it was November instead of October. Charles, though he had given Joan money for the poor of Bourges, had none for feeding and clothing his army. The town must have yielded soon, men thought, since no one came to succor it; but the French could neither besiege nor assault on empty stomachs, and the siege was abandoned. Charles, as a sugarplum to console the heartsick Maid, conferred a patent of nobility on her and all her family; "that the memory of the divine glory and of so many favors may endure and increase forever."

It was a pretty stone, to take the place of bread. A shining quartz pebble, shall we say? Or that curious thing called iron pyrite, which has been taken for gold before now, in a good light and by the right kind of person. Joan paid little heed to it; would never change her sacred devices, the Annunciation, the Crucifixion, the Creator on his throne, for any other; but her brothers set up a shield, with two lilies on it, and between these a sword supporting a crown. Yes, and they called themselves "Du Lys" instead of "D'Arc." This was all they got; I have not heard that the king so much as offered to pay for painting the new shield. The city of Orleans took a different view of matters, and endowed the mother of its own Maid with a pension which made her comfortable for life.

We know little of this winter of sorrow, the last in which Joan of Arc was to breathe free air. She spent part of it in Orleans, where the faithful people made much of her as usual; part at Mehun on the Yevre, where Charles kept his winter court. The truce with Burgundy had been extended to Easter 1430. John of Bedford had been kindly invited to share it, but declined, and kept up a lively guerilla warfare in Normandy. There was more or less fighting around Paris, too; but with that we have no special concern.

At Mehun there was nothing for Joan to do. She was no courtier; she was not wanted at the Councils over which the fatuous King and his fat favorite presided. Since Paris and La Charité, the crowd did not flock so eagerly to see her. Indeed, people began to talk about other wonderful women who appeared about this time. Catherine of La Rochelle, for example, had been visited by a lady in white and gold, who bade her ask the king for

heralds and trumpeters and go about the
country raising money. She had, it appeared,
the secret of finding hidden treasure. How,
people asked, if here were a new revelation?
The Maid's was an old story by this time.
Moreover, there were rumors of other Pucelles
here and there; and at Monlieu, as was well
known, lived a real saint, St. Colette, who
could make the sun rise three hours late, and
play—in a saintly way—the mischief with the
laws of Nature generally.

Our Maid was at Monlieu that very November; she may have met St. Colette, and talked
with her of matters human and divine; who
knows?

We do know that she met Catherine of La
Rochelle, who came to Mehun that autumn or
winter; and that she advised the lady to go
home, see to her household (she was a mar-
ried woman), and take care of her children
Catherine in return advised Joan not to go to
La Charité, "because it was much too cold."
Evidently, a lady who liked her little comforts.
Joan asked St. Catherine about her namesake,
and was told that her story was nonsense.
Still, the two women had much talk together.

The Rochellaise had high ambitions, was not in the least minded to go home to husband and children. She wanted to go in person to Philip of Burgundy and make peace; she wanted to prophesy for the king; like Nick Bottom, she would play the lion, too. Joan seems to have been patient with her; sat up all one night in her company, to see the lady in white and gold, who failed to appear. We need not concern ourselves further with Catherine of La Rochelle, though Brother Richard, the Franciscan, admired her greatly, and would fain have set her up on a pedestal beside Joan. She faded away presently, and is visible to-day only by a little reflected light from the flare of the Maid.

Winter came to an end at last, and with it the truce. Philip of Burgundy resumed hostilities, and Joan burnished her white armor, and laid her lance in rest with right good will. The end was near; all the more would she fight the good fight, so long as she was permitted.

About this time the people of Rheims wrote to her in great alarm, begging for help. Their captain had abandoned them, and gone no one knew whither. They had discovered a conspiracy, headed by Pierre Cauchon, Bishop of Beauvais and Joan's inveterate enemy, to deliver them up to the English. The discovery was made in time, but who could tell what new dangers might await them?

Joan wrote from Sully on March 16th, promising speedy help, and bidding them be of good heart, and man their walls in case of attack.

"You should have other good news," she says, "whereat you would rejoice, but I fear lest this fall into other hands."

A few days later she wrote again, assuring them that all Brittany was French at heart, and that its duke would shortly send to the king three thousand soldiers, paid two months in advance.

In late March or early April she took a new step. After months of waiting, after vigils of anguished prayer such as we can only feebly imagine, she decided to wait no longer for the king, but strike by herself one more blow for the country. She looked for no help of man; she had no encouragement from Heaven. Her Voices were not silent, but they spoke vaguely, confusedly; prophesied ultimate deliverance of

France, but said nothing of her being the deliverer; seemed dimly to hint at some forthcoming disaster.

Taking no leave of king or Council (although it seems probable that Charles knew of and consented to her departure), receiving no direction from saint or angel, she rode out from Sully with her "military household," four or five lances, among them her brothers and the ever-faithful D'Aulon. At Lagny she found a little band of men-at-arms who were ready to fight for France; they joined forces, and rode on toward Paris. There, the Maid always knew, lay the key of the situation; there, at what Philip of Burgundy called "the heart of the mystical body of the kingdom," the final blow must be struck.

The chronicles have little or nothing to say about this journey; we know that about Easter, April 16th, she came to Melun, and that the city, hearing of her approach, rose suddenly upon its Anglo-Burgundian garrison, drove them out of town, and opened wide its gates to the Maid. Here was good fortune indeed. Joan crossed the Seine, and entered the town amid general rejoicings. However it might be

in Royal Councils, the heart of France still
honored and loved its Pucelle.

After such deep and manifold humiliations,
Joan might well have been strengthened in
spirit as she stood on the ramparts of Melun
on a certain day in Easter week. Among the
many pictures of her, I like to conjure up this
one; to see her standing there, leaning on her
lance (she was on sentry duty), looking out
toward that "Isle of France" on whose edge
she now stood; no "isle" in reality, but the
quaintly-named province whose heart was
Paris. I can see her uplifted look, her kindling
eyes, can almost hear the deep-drawn breath
of high resolve and dedication.

And then the blow fell.

She had always known that her time was
short, that she had been given little more than
a year to fulfill her task; knew moreover, only
too bitterly well, how much of the short time
had been frittered away in spite of all her
efforts; yet she had hoped against hope that she
might be permitted to finish her allotted task.

The Voices, I have said, had been confused
of late; hinting at coming danger, but specify-
ing nothing. Now, as she stood on the rampart

of Melun that April day, they suddenly broke the silence, speaking loud and clear. No one but herself may tell the story; hear her tell it to her judges, a year later:

"As I was on the ramparts of Melun, St. Catherine and St. Margaret warned me that I should be captured before Midsummer Day; that so it must needs be; nor must I be afraid and astounded; but take all things well, for God would help me. So they spoke, almost every day. And I prayed that when I was taken I might die in that hour, without wretchedness of long captivity; but the Voices said that so it must be. Often I asked the hour, which they told me not; had I known the hour I would not have gone into battle." [1]

These were the same Voices that had called the peasant girl from her quiet home at Domrémy; the same that with trumpet note had sent her on from victory to victory, through the burning days of Orleans and Patay; now, as clear and loud, they pronounced her doom. She heard, and bowed her head before the heavenly will in meek acceptance.

Is not this perhaps the most wonderful part

[1] A Lang, p 203.

of all the heroic story? She never thought of escape; it never occurred to her to lay down the sword. If it had been so willed, she would have held her hand for one hour, would have kept her chamber at the moment of fate, if haply it might pass and leave her free for further effort; since that was not to be, forward, in God's name! There were still some good hours left.

Only one step higher, good Maid! that final step in Rouen Old Market, which shall take thee home to thy Father's house.

From Melun she rode to Lagny (whence the news of her presence spread to Paris, causing great alarm), and in that neighborhood had several skirmishes with the English, with little advantage to either side; and so, by-and-by, in mid-May, she came to Compiègne.

I make no apology for dwelling a little on these French towns which might—reverently be it said—be called the Stations of the Maid. Every rod of French ground is now and for all time sacred to us and to all lovers of Liberty.

Originally a hunting-lodge of the Frankish kings; the Romans called it Compendium.

COMPIÈGNE

Charles the Bald built two castles there, and a Benedictine abbey whose inmates received (and kept down to the 18th century), "the privilege of acting for three days as lords of Compiègne, with full power to release prisoners, condemn the guilty, and even inflict sentence of death."

The abbey church treasured the dust of three kings; possessed also a famous organ, the oldest in France, given by Constantine Copronymus (whoever he was!) to Pepin the Short. Louis the Debonair was deposed at Compiègne In its palace, Louis XV. received Marie Antoinette as his daughter-in-law, Napoleon I. received Marie Louise as his Empress. In the nineteenth century it was for many years the favorite resort of Napoleon III. and his court during the hunting season.

The memory pictures of this latter time are brilliant enough. Lovely Empresses, Eugenie with her matchless shoulders, Elizabeth, the "Violet of Austria" with her glorious hair, sweep through the famous forest in their long riding habits. Hunting horns sound the *morte* and the *hallali*, officers in scarlet and gold hold high counsel with others in gold and green.

All very gay, very bright; but these pictures shift and change like a kaleidoscope. Presently they vanish. Half a century passes, as a watch in the night. Compiègne looks from her girdling towers and sees a gray tide rush forward, seething and boiling, almost to her very walls; sees it met, stemmed, by a barrier of blue and brown, slender, but immovable; hears the words which shall ring through all centuries to come:

"*On ne passe pas!*"

Burgundy greatly desired Compiègne; would have had it before this, but for the stout hearts of its citizens. It was in Compiègne that the truce was signed, and Duke Philip asked explicitly that the city be given up to him while the compact held. Charles and La Trémoille were willing; anything to oblige! The citizens were bidden to open their gates to the soldiers of Burgundy. Their first answer was to bar and double-bar the said gates; their second, to send respectful messages to their king. They were his true and loyal subjects; their bodies and their possessions were his for all faithful service; but the duke of Burgundy hated them because of their loyalty to the king's Majesty, and they would in nowise let him in; would destroy themselves sooner.

The order was repeated; the gates remained closed. Philip of Burgundy stormed; Charles was very sorry, but did not see what he could do about it; offered Philip Pont St. Maxence instead. Philip took the gift, fully intending to have Compiègne too; and bided his time. He was busy that winter of 1429-30, marrying a new wife (his third, Isabella of Portugal), and founding the order of the Golden Fleece; all this with much pomp of tournament and procession. With spring came the end of the truce, and the duke took the field at once with a large army. Now he would have Compiègne, whether she would or no; would also overrun the Isle de France, and relieve Paris, which still went in fear of its life from the "Armagnacs," as Parisians still called the Royalist party.

Before the middle of May Philip was encamped before refractory Compiègne, with only the Oise between. Matters now marched swiftly. The Oise was deep, could not be forded; to take the city they must first take Choisy-le-Bac, on the opposite side of the

river, and come at Compiègne from the rear.
As it happened, the French about this time
were making a somewhat similar plan. They
meant to take Pont l'Evêque, now in English
hands, with its strong defences and its bridge
across the Oise. This secured, they too would
make a flank movement, circumvent the enemy,
and cut his line of communication across the
river.

On May 13th the Maid entered Compiègne
from the south, and was cordially received.
Here she met for the last time the Archbishop
of Rheims, her false friend, soon to become
her declared enemy. On the 14th she attacked
Pont l'Evêque, but the place was too strong
for her little band. On the 16th, Choisy-le-
Bac yielded to the Burgundians, and Joan returned to Compiègne. No thoroughfare!

Her only way now, as Burgundy had foreseen, was by the bridge of Soissons over the
Aisne, thirty miles and more away. To
Soissons, then, in God's name! She set out
without delay, the Archbishop riding with her,
and all her troop; reached Soissons—to find
the gates shut. The traitor who held the city
for France, a Picard, by name Bournel, was

even then making his arrangements with Burgundy. He refused to open the gates to his master's troops, and shortly after sold his city for four thousand *salus d'or*. The bill of sale is extant, and should be curious reading.

On meeting this check, the French army broke up into different parties. Joan determined to return to Compiègne; was already on her way thither when she heard that Burgundy and the Earl of Arundel were encamped before it. Her company was only two hundred men, commanded by one Baretta, a soldier of no wide renown. Alas! where was Dunois? Where La Hire, Xaintrailles? Where her friend and brother-in-arms, the gentle duke of Alençon? All gone! Some of them before Paris, keeping the Bourgeois and his like in daily terror of their lives; some, it may be, with their precious king, who about this time made the discovery (and told the people of Rheims, as an astounding piece of news!) that Burgundy did not really mean to make peace, and was definitely on the side of their enemies.

At midnight of May 22nd, the Maid left Crépy with her band, and rode rapidly through the forest. The soldiers themselves seem to

have been disheartened at the prospect before
them. "We are but a handful!" they told her.
"How can we pass through the armies of
England and Burgundy?"

"*Par mon martin!*" cried Joan; "we are
enough. I am going to see my good friends
at Compiègne."

That was a wild ride through the midnight
forest. Fancy, always at her tricks, tempts me
to make it even wilder; to tamper with the
Shuttle, and set the Loom astray. How if the
centuries should in some way juggle themselves
together, and the Nineteenth come sweeping
along with hound and horn before the eyes of
the Maid? What would she make, I wonder,
of those two lovely ladies, her of the shoulders
and her of the silken tresses? What in return
would they make of the slim rider in battered
armor, urging her horse to the gallop? They
would probably give orders to have her arrested for disturbing the royal sport.

But how if, instead of these, it might have
been given her, as part of her reward from
Heaven, to come upon that other band, in
armor not wholly unlike her own (seeing that
our To-day must needs snatch from Yesterday

anything and everything that may still avail to help); that band in brown and blue, who hold the line against the onrushing waves of the Gray Tide? How then? She scans the Line; her keen eyes lighten, then grow bewildered. France? Yes; but—England beside her? Friends then? Allies? *À la bonne heure!* The word?

"On ne passe pas!" and the Maid ranges herself beside those steadfast figures immovable; and "They" do not pass.

Shuttle and Loom to their proper places once more; back to May 22nd, 1430!

Joan was right Her little troop was enough, for no one molested them, the enemy not having yet reached that neighborhood. They came to Compiègne about sunrise of May 23rd, and once more were joyfully received.

How Joan spent that last fateful day we know not from any chronicle; we may be sure that she prayed, and heard mass if mass were to hear; we may hope she had some rest, for she needed it sorely. We may well believe, too, that she listened for her Voices, hoping for counsel and—if it might be—cheer; but the Voices were silent. She was alone now.

Nevertheless, she said afterward, had the heavenly counsellors bidden her go out, saying plainly that she would be captured, she would still have gone. In another mood, it is true, after imprisonment, and with death close upon her, she thought that had she known the hour, she might have kept her chamber during it; but the first is the true mood, for all who know her.

At five in the afternoon she rode out to attack the nearest Burgundian outpost, at the village of Margny, opposite the bridge-head on the northern side of the river. Boldly she rode her gray charger, in full armor, wearing a surcoat of scarlet and gold, followed by her four or five hundred men-at-arms, horse and foot. The enemy, taken by surprise, scattered in disorder. All might have gone well, had not John of Luxembourg, commander of Flemings at Clairoix hard by, chosen this moment to visit the Burgundian captain in charge of Margny. Seeing the skirmish, and his brother officer in difficulties, he dashed to the rescue, sending back meanwhile to his own camp for reinforcements. Another moment and the tide had turned. The French were surrounded, set upon, cut down, routed. The Maid tried desperately to rally them; cried her brave battle cry, waved her shining standard. What mortal could do, she did.

"Beyond the nature of woman," says Chastellain, the Burgundian chronicler, "she did great feats, and took great pains to save her company from loss, staying behind them like a captain, and like the bravest of the troop." Twice she charged the men of Luxembourg and drove them back. In vain! the hour was come.

She was alone now, save for her brothers, d'Aulon, and the faithful few, her bodyguard. These could not save her. Round her, like hounds about a deer at bay, leaped and shouted the Burgundian soldiers, all eager for the rich quarry. She was dragged from her horse, beaten to earth. D'Aulon and the rest tried to help her up, but were overwhelmed by numbers and made prisoners, every man of them.

"Yield thee, Pucelle!" cried a dozen voices, as a dozen brawny hands clutched the slight form and held it fast, fast.

Joan raised herself, and looked round on her exulting foes, conquered yet unafraid.

"I have pledged my faith to Another than you!" she said. "To Him I will keep my oath."

So to the will of God she surrendered, who had never yielded to man, and laid down at His feet her glorious sword.

.

CHAPTER XVI

ROUEN

"Bishop of Beauvais! because the guilt-burthened man
is in dreams haunted by the most frightful of his crimes
.. you also, entering your final dream, saw Domrémy.
... My lord, have you no counsel? 'Counsel I have
none; in heaven above, or on earth beneath, counsellor
there is none now that would take a brief from *me*, all
are silent.'

"Is it, indeed, come to this? Alas! the time is short,
the tumult is wondrous, the crowd stretches away into
infinity, but yet I will search in it for somebody to take
your brief; I know of somebody that will be your counsel
Who is this that cometh from Domrémy? Who is she
that cometh in bloody coronation robes from Rheims?
Who is she that cometh with blackened flesh from walk-
ing the furnaces of Rouen? This is she, the shepherd
girl, counsellor that had none for herself, whom I choose,
Bishop, for yours. She it is, I engage, that shall take
my lord's brief. She it is, Bishop, that would plead for
you, yes, Bishop, SHE—when heaven and earth are
silent "

—De Quincey

WE need not dwell upon the joy of English
and Burgundians, or of their French
sympathizers: it was as rapturous as it was
savage. John of Luxembourg, a typical soldier

239

of fortune, had but one idea, that of turning his prisoner to good account. Who would pay most for her?

While the matter was pending, Joan was hurried from castle to castle, from prison to prison. Clairoix, the headquarters of Luxembourg, was not strong enough to hold her; she might escape, or there might be a rescue. She was sent to Beaulieu, and thence to Beaurevoir, where she stayed from June to September. Here she was in the kind hands of three ladies, all bearing her own name; Jeanne of Luxembourg, aunt of her captor; Jeanne of Bethune, Viscountess of Meaux, his wife, and her daughter Jeanne of Bar. These good ladies befriended the captive Maid: gave her the last womanly comfort and tendance she was to receive; begged her to put on woman's dress, and brought stuff to make it. Joan was grateful, but shook her head. She had no leave yet from God to do this: the time was not come. She would have done it, she said later, had her duty permitted, for these ladies rather than for any soul in France except her queen.

Harmond de Macy, a knight who saw the Maid at Beaurevoir and who offered her familiarities which she gravely repulsed, has left his impressions of her on record.

"She was of honest conversation in word and deed," he says: and adds at the end of his testimony, given after her death, "I believe she is in paradise."

Joan would give no parole. She steadfastly maintained her right to escape if she might. Here at Beaurevoir she made her one attempt to do so, moved thereto largely by anxiety for the people of Compiègne, now besieged. She was told that if the town were taken all the people over seven years of age would be put to death. This she could not bear. In vain her Voices dissuaded her: in vain St. Catherine almost daily forbade it. "I would rather die than live," said the Maid, "after such a massacre of good people."

Evading her jailers one day, she leapt from the tower, a height of sixty feet. Wonderful to relate, no bones were broken, but she was found insensible, and taken back to prison. For several days she could neither eat nor drink. Then, she told her judges later, St. Catherine comforted her, bidding her make confession and ask God's forgiveness for the leap. The saint told her that Compiègne would be relieved before Martinmas, as in fact came to pass.

"Then," she says, "I revived, and took food, and soon was well."

She denied having expected death from the leap: she had hoped to escape, partly to help Compiègne, partly because she was sold to the English.

"I would rather die," she said, "than fall into the hands of my English enemies "

She was to do both. English and French were of one mind. The former were headed (in this matter) by the Earl of Warwick, the latter by Pierre Cauchon, Bishop of Beauvais This man had been disappointed, through Joan's successes, in certain private ambitions. He pursued her from first to last with incredible fury and persistence; it was through his efforts that John of Luxembourg was enabled to sell her (despite the earnest prayers of the aged Jeanne de Luxembourg) to England for ten thousand livres; it was he who conducted her trial and brought her to her death

From Beaurevoir she was taken to Arras; thence, after one night at the castle of Drugy, to Crotoy by the sea: and so, in November of 1430, she came to Rouen.

They took her to the old castle built by Philip Augustus in 1205; used in the days of the English occupation as a prison for "prisoners of war and treasonable felons." Of this structure, with its six towers, demi-tower and donjon, only one vestige remains, the *"Tour Jeanne d'Arc,"* a bulk of solid masonry one hundred feet high, forty feet in diameter, with walls twelve feet thick. You may visit it to-day; may stand in the dark cell, and see the iron cage in which, according to some authorities, the Maid was at first confined. During most of the time she was chained to a log of wood, her fetters loosened only when she was taken into court. She was guarded day and night by English men-at-arms, most of them common and brutal soldiers. She had no moment of solitude, no shadow of privacy. Her days were anguish, her nights terror; yet though her gaolers jeered, bullied, baited her with every foul jest and bitter insult, she kept the virgin treasure of her soul and of her body.

One day the Earls of Stafford and Warwick came to see her, and with them John of Luxembourg who sold her, and Haimond de Macy. The latter tells of the interview, saying that Luxembourg offered to ransom her if she would swear never to bear arms again.

"In God's name, you mock me!" said the Maid. "I know well that you have neither the will nor the power."

Luxembourg repeating his offer, she put him aside with: "I know these English will put me to death, thinking to win the kingdom of France when I am no more. But were they a hundred thousand more *Godons* than they are, they should not have the kingdom."

At this Stafford drew his dagger and would have stabbed her (she, poor soul, asking no better!), but Warwick held his hand. This latter noble, son-in-law of Warwick, the king-maker, and called by some "the Father of Courtesy," was eager for the burning of Joan; it was, in his opinion, the only fitting end for her. No clean stab of an honorable dagger for the witch of the Armagnacs!

So we come to the Trial, about which so many books have been written; over which churchmen and statesmen, French and English, have wrangled through nigh upon six hundred years. I shall dwell on it so much as seems absolutely necessary, and no more.

On January 9th, 1431, Pierre Cauchon, Bishop of Beauvais, master of the bloodhounds in this glorious hunt, summoned his council. There were two judges, the bishop himself and Le Maître, Vice Inquisitor in the diocese of Rouen. The latter, after the first month, sat unwillingly; his conscience was not clear; he would fain be rid of the whole matter. The orders of the Chief Inquisitor, however, were strict; he sat on, ill at ease. The rest of the Council were clerks and "assessors"; all clerics of name and fame, canons of Rouen, abbots, learned doctors. You may easily learn their names, yet methinks they are best forgotten. Their number varied from day to day; sometimes there were forty, again there would be but six; most of them were French, but there were one or two Englishmen among them.

On February 20th, Joan of Arc, known as the Maid, was summoned to appear before this Council. She begged to be allowed to hear mass first, but was refused. On the 21st, she was brought before her judges in the chapel of the castle.

We may fancy the scene   Priests and prelates in goodly array of furred robes, episcopal crosses, and the like, sitting in half-circle, with bent brows and grim looks. Before their scandalized eyes, a slim girl in page's dress of black, her dark hair cut short, her face worn with watching and fasting, white with prison pallor.

She is accused of witchcraft, and dealings with familiar spirits; of wearing man's clothes (see them on the wench this moment!) ; of attacking Paris; of attempting suicide, of allowing ignorant people to worship her as a saint or holy person, of stealing a bishop's horse; of pretending to work miracles   One or two other charges were added in the course of the trial to this heavy list

To begin with, the prisoner was commanded to give a full account of herself and her pretended mission. Joan was prepared for this The Voices were with her in prison throughout the trial, counseling, warning, consoling. Sometimes she merely felt the blessed presences about her; sometimes they spoke plainly, even dictating her answers; always bidding her "answer boldly and God would help her."

Called upon to be sworn, she refused to take an unqualified oath. She did not know on what subjects they might question her.

"You may ask me things which I will not tell you. As to revelations to my King I will not speak though you should cut off my head."

She finally took a qualified oath, agreeing to speak plainly on such subjects as her conscience allowed. She would not repeat the Lord's Prayer (a favorite test of witchcraft; a witch, as everyone knew, could only say it backward!), save in confession; she would in no wise swear or promise to refrain from trying to escape; she had given no *parole*, and it was the right of every prisoner. She answered readily enough the questions concerning her birth, parentage, and so on.

She was interrupted every moment by some fresh question or rebuke. The notary Manchon, who was reporting the meeting, refused to act if things were not better ordered; he was an honest man, and reported Joan's words correctly, which was not the case with some other clerks present.

On the second day she came fasting to her trial, for it was Lent. She had eaten but once the day before. Massieu, the doorkeeper, seems to have been, like the notary, a decent man, and was wont to let her stop and pray on her way from cell to chapel, before the door of the chapel. One Estivet, a prison spy (*mouton*), and tool of Cauchon's, rebuked him fiercely for this leniency. "Rascal," he said, "how dare you let that excommunicate wretch come so near the church? If you persist, you shall be shut up yourself, in a tower where you shall not see sun or moon for a month."

Massieu, according to his own account, paid no heed to this threat, but continued to allow the Maid to kneel before the closed door of the holy place.

On the third day, after long and puerile questionings about the supposititious fairies of her childhood and the Voices of her early girl-hood, she was asked suddenly, "Do you consider that you are in a state of grace?"

Here was a good strong trap, well laid and baited. If she answered "Yes," she was guilty of presumption in holy matters; if "No," her own mouth spoke her condemnation.

Quietly the Maid uttered what her historian calls her inspired reply. "If I am not in grace, may God bring me thither; if I am, God keep me there."[1]

Considering her steadfast and valiant bearing throughout these days of trial, we may well believe that the God she adored gave her strength and constancy. She had no earthly friend. The only person who visited her in the guise of human kindness was a spy of the Inquisition, one Loiseleur, a canon of Chartres and Rouen, and a close friend and ally of Cauchon. This base wretch, set on by his chief and the Earl of Warwick, did visit the Maid in her cell, in accordance with a mandate of the Inquisition which reads: "Let no one approach the heretic, unless it be from time to time two faithful and skilful persons, who shall act as if they had pity on him, and shall warn him to save himself by confessing his errors, promising him, if he does so, that he shall not be burned."

Loiseleur came in layman's dress, telling Joan that he was a man of Lorraine, her friend and that of France. He was full of interest

[1] Translation, A Lang

and solicitude. The Voices gave no warning, and the lonely girl talked with him far more freely than with her judges. He would gently lead the subject to some point which was to be brought up the next day, and on his report the Council would frame its questions. Manchon, the notary, was asked to establish himself in a closet hard by, where he could hear and take down the words of the prisoner; this, to his lasting honor, he indignantly refused to do, saying he would report what was said in open court and nothing else.

The days dragged on, and the weeks; weeks of prayer, of fasting, of torment. On March 14th she was interrogated concerning her leap from the tower of Beaurevoir. Was it true that after her fall she had blasphemed God and her saints?

Not of her consciousness, she replied. "God and good confession" knew; she had no knowledge of what she might have said in delirium. St. Catherine had promised her help, how or when she knew not.

"Generally, the Voices say that I shall be delivered through great victory; and furthermore they say, 'Take all things peacefully;

heed not thine affliction. Thence thou shalt come at last into the kingdom of Paradise.'"

The judges took up this question delightedly; it was one after their own hearts. Did she, they asked, feel assurance of salvation?

"As firmly as if I were in heaven already."

"Do you believe that, *after this revelation,* you could not sin mortally?"

"I know not. I leave it to God."

"Your answer (about her assurance of salvation) is very weighty."

"I hold it for a very great treasure."

"What with your attack on Paris on a holy day, your behavior in the matter of the Bishop's hackney, your leap at Beaurevoir, and your consent to the death of Franquet, do you really believe that you have wrought no mortal sin?"

"I do not believe that I am in mortal sin; and if I have been it is for God to know it, and for confession to God and the priest."[1]

She begged to be allowed to go to church. If she might hear mass she would wear woman's dress, changing it on her return for the page's dress which was her protection

[1] Trans, A Lang

against insult. If she must die, she asked for a woman's shift, and a cap to cover her head; she would rather die than depart from the work for which her Lord had sent her.

"But I do not believe," she added, "that my Lord will let me be brought so low that I shall lack help of God and miracle."

"If you dress as you do by God's command," they asked her, "why do you ask for a shift in the hour of death?"

"It suffices me that it should be long!" said the girl.

All this was but the preliminary inquiry. Now followed a week of respite, while the evidence was sifted and arranged, and articles of indictment drawn up. On March 27th Joan was summoned to hear her formal accusation, conveyed in seventy articles. The Court was asked to declare her "a sorceress, a divineress, a false prophet, one who invoked evil spirits, a witch, a heretic, an apostate, a seditious blasphemer, rejoicing in blood, indecent," and I know not what else beside. These seventy articles were presently condensed into twelve. On April 6th the learned doctors were called to deliberate on these twelve, which constituted the real accusation, by which the captive must live or die.

They met in the private chapel of the Archbishop, which is still standing, in the courtyard hard by the cathedral. The articles were duly accepted, and the Maid was summoned to hear the result. But she lay ill in her prison, worn out with fasting and misery. Cauchon himself came to visit her, professing himself full of tender solicitude for her soul and body. He bade her note how kind they were to her. They desired only her welfare; the Holy Church was ever ready to receive its erring children, etc., etc. With her unfailing courtesy Joan thanked him. She thought herself in danger of death; she begged for confession and the sacrament, and burial in holy ground.

"If you desire the Holy Sacrament," said Cauchon, "you must submit to Holy Church."

The girl turned her head wearily on her pallet. "I can say no more than I have said!" was her only word.

But the Bishop pressed on relentless. The more she feared for her life, he told her, the more she would resolve to amend it, and submit to those above her. Then she said:

"If my body dies in prison I expect from you burial in holy ground; if you do not give it, I await upon my Lord." And as they still tormented her:

"Come what may, I will do or say no other thing. I have answered to everything in my trial."

Five Doctors in turn beset her with offers of favors if she would yield, with threats if she continued obdurate. In the latter case, they told her, she must be treated as a Saracen. Finally, since they might in no wise prevail over the dauntless soul, though the broken body lay helpless before them, they departed, leaving her to the tenderer mercies of the men-at-arms.

The Articles of Accusation had been sent to the University of Paris, with a request for the opinion of that learned and pious body. While waiting for the answer, the Bishop of Beauvais filled the time with various ingenious devices, all planned to break the girl's spirit. On May 2nd, being in some measure recovered from her illness, she was brought out for a public meeting before sixty clerics, Cauchon at their head. The Bishop addressed her in his customary strain, accusing, exhorting, admonishing.

"Read your book!" (i.e., the document containing her formal accusation), said Joan scornfully. "I will answer as I may. My appeal is to God, my Creator, whom I love with my whole heart."

Wearily, wearily she listened to the many-times-told tale; briefly and bravely she made reply.

"If I were now at the judgment seat, and if I saw the torch burning, and the fagots laid, and the executioner ready to light the fire; if I were in the fire, I would say what I have said, and no other word; would do what I have done, and no other thing."

"*Superba responsio!*" writes Manchon the clerk opposite this entry.

Since naught else might prevail against the obstinacy of this creature, how if they tried torture, or at the very least the threat of torture, the actual sight of its instruments?

Two days later (May 4th), she was brought out again, this time into a dismal vaulted chamber, the donjon of Rouen Castle. The usual place of her torment was too small for the things she now saw displayed before her; rack, screws, all the hideous paraphernalia of the Holy Inquisition; beside these, two executioners, ready to perform their office.

Joan was bidden to look upon these things, and told that if she did not avow the truth her body would be submitted to the torture. If we stood, as one may still stand, in that vaulted chamber, would not the answer ring out once more from those grim walls that received it?

"Truly, if you should destroy my limbs and cause my soul to leave my body, I will tell you no other thing (than she has already told); and if I should say anything (i.e., under torture), I would always tell you afterward that you had made me say it by force."

She trod, indeed, the narrow edge of a knife-blade. Question upon question was put; was answered briefly, clearly, and to the point. The clerics hesitated. Perhaps the torture might not be necessary, since there seemed a chance that even this might not prevail against this girl's stubbornness. In any case it would be well to leave the fear of it hanging over her for a time.

It was so left, for a week, while the doctors

debated. One thought the use of torture might "impair the stately beauty of the trial as hitherto conducted." Another thought they had sufficient evidence without it. Three were in favor of it: Morelli, Courcelles, Loiseleur. The last-named was the Judas-spy who had visited her in prison; he thought torture would be salutary for her soul. After all, this particular depth of infamy was not sounded; the votes for mercy outnumbered those for torture. The executioner and his henchmen departed, the former testifying later that the Maid "showed great prudence in her replies, so that those who heard were astonished; and their deponent retired with his assistant without touching her."

Still another week of fetters and darkness, of foul air and fouler speech; then came the reply from the University of Paris. They rejoiced in the "elegance" with which the crime of this person had been communicated to them. It was clear to their minds that her pretended saints were in reality three well-known fiends, Satan, Belial, and Behemoth. She was treacherous, cruel, bloodthirsty, a would-be suicide; a liar, heretic, schismatic and idolater. Nevertheless, in the opinion of the University, it might be well to give her one more "tender admonition." It could do no harm; the English were safe to deal with her in any case.

On May 23rd she received the admonition—it really seems to have been a kindly one this time—from Pierre Maurice, who appealed to her sense of honor and duty.

"What," he asked her, "would you think of a knight in your king's land who refused to obey your king and his officers? Yet you, a daughter of the Church, disobey the officers of Christ, the bishops of the Church. Be not ashamed of obedience, have no false shame; you will have high honor, which you think you will lose, if you act as I ask you to do. *The honor of God* and your own life in this world, and your salvation in the next, are to be preferred before all things." [1]

Joan made no answer to this appeal, but it may have had its effect none the less.

The next day, May 24th, she was placed in a tumbril and brought to the market-place of St. Ouen, where a great crowd was assembled;

[1] Trans, A Lang

priests, nobles, soldiers, citizens, all agog to see and hear. Would she abjure, or burn?

It was customary to preach a final sermon to a witch before burning her; Erard, the preacher, addressed Joan this morning. In the course of his speech he spoke of the king as a "heretic and schismatic."

"*Speak boldly!*" said the holy Voices in the ear of the Maid.

"By my faith," she cried, "full well dare I both say and swear that he is the noblest Christian of all Christians, and the truest lover of the faith and the Church."

Charles, were I set to devise for you a fitting doom, I would have you loiter through some dim place of forgotten things—not forever, but as near it as Divine Mercy would allow— seeing always before you the pale Maid in her fetters, hearing always from her lips those words of undying trust and love.

Enough; the matter was summed up. Here was the executioner, here his cart, ready to carry her to the stake. Would Joan of Arc submit to Holy Church, or would she burn, now, in an hour's time?

You are to remember that this child was not

yet nineteen years of age; that she had been
in prison, enduring every torment except that
of actual bodily torture, for a year. To remember, too, that even our Supreme Exemplar
prayed once that the cup might pass from him.

"I submit!" said the Maid.

Instantly a paper was thrust into her hand,
and she was bidden sign it. Bystanders say
there was a strange smile on her lips as she
made her mark, a circle, as we know she could
not write her name. She was hustled back to
prison, leaving tumult and uproar behind her.
The English were furious. They had come to
see a burning, and there was no burning.
Warwick made complaint to Cauchon; the
King of England would be angry at the escape
of this witch.

"Be not disturbed, my Lord!" said the
Bishop of Beauvais. "We shall soon have her
again."

Back to prison! not, as she had hoped and
prayed, to a prison of the Church, where men
whose profession at least was holy would be
about her; where possibly she might even see
and speak with a woman; where she might hear
mass, and make confession. No! back to the

old foul, hideous cell, to the brutal jeer and fleer of the English men-at-arms. Back, under sentence of imprisonment for life.

Meekly the poor girl went; meekly she put off her page's costume, and assumed, as she was bidden, a woman's dress.

On some aspects of the dark days that followed I cannot dwell; suffice it to say that they were the bitterest of all the bitter year; suffice it to say that when her judges came to her again they found her once more in her page's dress, which she refused to give up again until the end.

This was not the only change they found, nor the greatest. Back in the cell, the Voices had spoken loud and clear in rebuke and reproach. St. Margaret, St. Catherine, both were there. Both told her of the great pity of that betrayal to which she had consented, when she made that abjuration and revocation to save her life; told her that by so doing she had condemned herself.

"If I were to say" (it is herself speaking now) "that God did not send me I would condemn myself, for true it is that God sent me. My Voices have told me since that I greatly

JOAN OF ARC

sinned in that deed, in confessing that I had
done ill. What I said, I said in fear of fire." [1]

And the clerk wrote against these words, on
the margin of his notes, "*Responsio Morti-
fera.*"

The Maid now clearly and emphatically re-
voked her submission. What she had said, she
repeated, was said in dread of fire.

"Do you believe," asked Cauchon, "that
your Voices are those of St. Catherine and St.
Margaret?"

"Yes!" replied the Maid. "Their voices
and God's!"

These words were spoken on May 28th, to
Cauchon, who had hastened to the prison,
hearing that Joan had resumed man's apparel.
Angrily he asked why she had done this. She
answered that it was more convenient, among
men, to wear men's dress. She had not understood that she had sworn never to wear it
again; if she had broken a pledge in this, one
had been broken with her, the promise that she
should be released from fetters, and should
receive the sacrament.

"I would rather die," she said, "than remain

[1] Trans, A Lang

262

ROUEN

in irons. If you will release me, and let me
go to mass and lie in gentle prison, I will be
good, and do what the Church desires."

There was only one thing that the Church,
as represented in the person of Pierre Cauchon,
desired, and that was the end of her. She had
"relapsed"; it was enough. He hurried joyfully away, passing in the courtyard Warwick
and his men, who were waiting for news.

"Farewell!" cried the Bishop of Beauvais.
"Be of good cheer, for it is done."

He summoned his Council in haste; they
were all of his mind. Holy Church could have
no further dealings with this impious and
hardened prisoner. She must be given over to
the secular arm, "with the prayer that there
be no shedding of blood." Most sinister of all
speakable words! At the stake, no need of
blood-shedding.

Early in the morning of May 29th Martin
Ladvenu and Jean Toutmouillé came to the
prison. The latter told the Maid briefly that
she was to be burned. She wept, poor child,
and cried out piteously.

"Alas!" she said. "Will they treat me so
horribly and cruelly, that my pure and uncor-

rupted body (*"corps net et entier, qui ne fut jamais corrompu"*) must to-day be burned to ashes?"

She would rather, she cried in her agony, be seven times beheaded than burn.

"I appeal to God, the supreme Judge, against the wrongs that have been done me."

At this moment Cauchon entered the prison. He must see with his own eyes how his victim received her condemnation. She turned upon him, and uttered the words which, wherever his name is spoken, whenever his image is conjured up, are written in flame upon his forehead:

"Bishop of Beauvais, it is through you I die. I summon you before your God and mine!"

Presently she composed herself; made confession to one of the monks, and asked for the Sacrament. After some haggling among her persecutors the elements were brought to her, albeit in slovenly fashion, bare of the priestly pomp which was their due.

So we come to the 30th day of May, of the year 1431. At nine in the morning Joan left her prison for the last time. She was in woman's dress. Over her shoulders was the long black robe of the Inquisition, on her head a paper cap or mitre, bearing the words: "Heretic, Relapsed, Apostate, Idolater." As the cart in which she stood rumbled through the streets, the Maid of France lifted up her voice and wept over the city of her death.

"Rouen, Rouen, mourrai-je içi? Seras-tu ma maison? Ah, Rouen, j'ai grand peur que tu n'aies à souffrir de ma mort." [1]

Hearing these words, the people around her, even the English soldiers, wept for pity. It is recorded that as the tumbril jolted its way over the stones, a man in priest's dress was seen pressing through the crowd, trying desperately to force a way to the cart. It was Loiseleur, the spy, come in an agony of repentance, to fling himself before the saint he had helped to condemn and implore her pardon. The soldiers repulsed him brutally; would have slain him but for Warwick's intervention. The crowd closed over him.

There were three scaffolds in Rouen Old Market that morning of May. On one of

[1] Rouen, Rouen, shall I die here? Shalt thou be my (last) home? Ah, Rouen, I have great fear thou must suffer for my death

them the Maid was set to hear her last sermon preached by Nicholas Midi, of Rouen and Paris; on another sat judges and spectators, a goodly company; Cardinal Beaufort, Warwick, the "Father of Courtesy," Cauchon and all his priestly bloodhounds, who yet could not see blood shed.

The third scaffold was a heap of plaster, piled high with fagots, from which rose the stake. It bore the legend: "Jeanne, self-styled the Maid, liar, mischief-maker, abuser of the people, diviner, superstitious, blasphemer of God, presumptuous, false to the faith of Christ, boaster, idolater, cruel, dissolute, an invoker of devils, apostate, schismatic, heretic."

Nicholas Midi was long in speaking, and the English waxed impatient. Dinner time was near.

"How now, priest? Are you going to make us dine here?" some of them cried.

Cauchon read the sentence.

"Then she invoked the blessed Trinity, the glorious Virgin Mary, and all the blessed saints of Paradise. She begged right humbly also the forgiveness of all sorts and conditions of men, both of her own party and of her enemies;

asking for their prayers, forgiving them the evil that they had done her." [1]

The Bailiff of Rouen waved his hand, saying "Away with her." ·

Quietly, patiently, the Maid climbed the third scaffold. She was well used to climbing, witness the walls of Les Tourelles, of Jargeau and Compiègne. Beside her climbed her confessor, Martin Ladvenu, and some say another Dominican, Isambart de la Pierre, who had been kind to her throughout. She begged for a cross; an English soldier hastily bound two sticks together cross-fashion and handed her the emblem. She kissed it devoutly, and thrust it in her bosom. Then, at her urgent prayer, they brought a crucifix from a church hard by; this she long embraced, holding it while they chained her to the stake.

When the flames began to mount, she bade the friar leave her, but begged him to hold aloft the crucifix, that her eyes might rest on it to the last. This man testified that from the heart of the fire, she called steadfastly on her Saints, Catherine, Margaret, Michael, as if

[1] Trans, A Lang.

they were once more about her as in the garden of Domrémy.

"To the end she maintained that her Voices were from God, and all she had done was by God's counsel; nor did she believe that her Voices had deceived her."

At the last she gave one great cry: "Jesus!" and spoke no more.

Have you felt the touch of fire? Put your finger in the candle flame for a moment! Then, for another moment—not more, since that way madness lies—think of that white, tender body of the Maid of France flaming like a torch to Heaven!

A torch indeed. Fiercely its blaze beats upon Rouen Old Market, throwing a dreadful light on those watching faces. Pierre de Cauchon, Bishop of Beauvais, on your face it glares most fiercely; on yours, Henry Beaufort, Cardinal of Winchester; Earl of Warwick, on yours. I think you will see that light while you live, however dark the night around you. I know that by it alone we see your faces to-day.

A torch, indeed. Its flame brightens the sacred fields of France, now in the hour of Vic-

ROUEN

tory, when light has triumphed over darkness.
as it brightened them in the hour of her agony,
though God alone saw that radiance. In the
white fire of that torch were fused all inco-
herent elements, all that turned the sword of
brother against brother, Frenchman against
Frenchman. From that white fire sprang, into
enduring life and glory, France Imperishable.

FINIS

Lightning Source UK Ltd.
Milton Keynes UK
UKOW042042050313

207199UK00001B/89/A